CW00670579

theProperty Makeover Price Guide:

Organising & Budgeting for Home Improvers & Developers
2nd Edition

The Building Cost Information Service

The Property Makeover Price Guide
Organising and Budgeting for Home Improvers and Developers
2nd Edition

©BCIS 2008

ISBN 978 1 904829 80 5

BCIS
12 Great George Street
Parliament Square
London SW1P 3AD

www.bcis.co.uk

BCIS is the Building Cost Information Service of RICS

Printed in Wales by Print Direction Ltd, Llanmaes, Wales www.printdirection.co.uk

All rights reserved. No part of this publication may be reproduced, stored in a retrieval system, or transmitted in any form or by any means, electronic, mechanical, photocopying, recording or otherwise without the prior permission of the Copyright owner.

While all reasonable care has been taken in the compilation of this document, BCIS, the Royal Institution of Chartered Surveyors and the compilers will not be under any legal liability in respect of any mis-statement, error or omission contained therein or for the reliance any person may place thereon.

the Property Makeover Price Guide

Contents

1.4 Planning and Building Legislation and Regulations

1.5 Major Property Problems

Part 2

2.1 Repairs

2.2 Services

2.3 Finishes

Preface

The first edition of the Property Makeover Guide was well received by the general public.

Prices have been rising sharply in the small contractor market and differentially for the various specialist trades. This has required a thorough revision and updating of the prices for this new edition.

We have now added a section on weather damage, which brings together typical items of repairs and their costs for storm, flood, snow and earthquake damage.

Following requests from users of the Guide, we have expanded the information included in Part One. Additional information is provided on Building Regulations including replacement windows and doors, Competent Persons Self Certification Schemes and asbestos removal. Information has also been included on Home Information Packs and recommendations for regular maintenance audits of your property.

We are keen to hear your comments on the Guide and any suggestions for additions and improvements, so that we can continue to improve its content and coverage in future editions.

PART ONE

1.1 INTRODUCTION

Introduction

This guide will help you if you want to:

- Do up a property and sell it
- Improve your own home
- Fix a problem with your home

There are lots of books available telling you what to do to improve your property. What they don't usually tell you is what it will really cost. This guide does.

The guide:

- Gives you the cost information that will enable you to budget for repair, improvement, alteration and extension work, and
- Walks you through how to obtain builders or specialist contractors to actually do the work.

A Cautionary Tale

If you've watched any of the TV home makeover and property development programmes you'll know that it is very important to get your budget right before starting any construction project.

Some of the TV makeover programmes only talk about the costs of materials. If you were to run some of these projects yourself, you would need to budget the cost of all those workmen 'the labour' and what it would cost you to get advice from the 'TV experts'.

On the development programmes, the budgets set by the participants are often too low.

- The cost of good design work is underestimated.
- They expect a higher quality than their budgets will allow.
- Generally, they are over optimistic about what you can get for your money.

Repairs – 'a stitch in time saves nine'

With repairs, the stitch in time saying certainly applies. The main rule in looking after a property is to ensure that you carry out repairs before small defects lead to serious problems and therefore major costs.

When doing up a property for sale it is important that you get the basics right before upgrading the decorations and fittings. Or, in other words, there is no point putting in a new bathroom if the roof is dodgy and will leak in the first heavy rain of winter.

The guide gives you advice on

- The types of work you may need to undertake when doing up a property, together with approximate costs.
- An idea of the costs for alteration and repair work.
- Costs for a range of new extensions, porches, conservatories, garden rooms and garages.

There is also guidance on:

- Selecting contractors.
- How to carry out the work.
- Deciding payment - what to pay, to whom and when.
- Changing your mind - what to do if you want to ask for something different to be carried out - variations and extras.

There are common pitfalls in all these areas and this guide will help keep you out of trouble.

You may be able to get grants from your local authority for renovation work. This guide explains the eligibility, the limits and how to apply them. It is worth a look but the reality is that unless you are on a low income, you are unlikely to be eligible.

Layout of the Guide

This guide is in four parts:

Part One

- Introduction
- Layout of the guide
- How to use the guide
- Major property problems
- Extensions and alterations to the property
- How to employ a contractor
- Planning and building legislation and regulations to consider before undertaking the work, particularly with regards to works of alteration and new works
- Party walls, building materials and grants.

Part Two

The main part of the guide contains the cost information on items of repair, alterations, and new works.

- Items of Repair
  o Work to the fabric of the property
  o Services
  o Finishes
  o Redecoration

- Common alteration work
  o Reroofing the property
  o Forming openings within the building
  o Retiling walls
  o Replacing flooring
  o Replacing doors and fireplaces
  o Replacing sanitary suites and heating systems
  o New drain runs and manholes.

- New works - total project costs
  o New extensions
  o Conservatories
  o Garden rooms
  o Loft and basement conversions
  o New porches
  o Garages and car ports

  o Kitchen replacement
  o Bathroom replacement.
- Damage by weather or earthquake

Part Three

- Costing assumptions used in build up of the prices in this guide
- General building information
- Useful contacts.

Glossary

The glossary will help you talk to the builder. The cost information is described in terms that a builder understands. Of course this means that there will be some items where you may say 'well what on earth is that'. The glossary will help you to get around this problem.

How to Use the Guide

For any building project you should follow some simple steps:

1. Identify the work required.
2. Consult specialists where appropriate.
3. Produce a budget.
4. Consult a contractor(s).
5. Adjust your budget for any additional work identified.
6. Obtain quotes.
7. Agree payment schedule.
8. Commence work.

Part 1.2 of the guide shows how the information has been presented and suggests how it can be used.

It is important that you read the Introduction in full before trying to use the costs in this guide on a specific project of repair, alteration or extension work.

1.2 COST INFORMATION

About the Cost Information
The cost information in Part Two is in seven sections.

1. Repairs
This covers most of the items of repair work that you will need to do to the existing fabric of the property.

They have been identified as defects:
- eg 'window is damaged or rotten'

With a solution:
- eg 'replace window'

And guide prices for various types and sizes of window
- eg timber casement window
  600 x 900mm - £545

The cost will apply equally if you decide to replace the windows for aesthetic rather than practical reasons ie you just don't like them.

2. Services
This section includes all repair work to water, electricity and heating installations.

3. Finishes
This section provides costs for repairing and replacing floor, wall and ceiling finishes within the property.

4. Redecorations
This provides prices for repainting walls, ceilings, doors, windows and woodwork.

5. Common alterations works and indicative costs
These cover work you may do to change the way a property works eg forming openings, or installing false ceilings, replacing the heating system, or a bathroom suite.

6. Total project costs
This section provides prices for extensions, conservatories, etc and for replacing a kitchen or bathroom including fittings and equipment.

7. Weather damage and earthquake
This covers work that may be required as a result of storm, flood, snow or earthquake damage.

What is Included in the Costs
The costs given in all the tables include for everything necessary to carry out the works. This includes:
- Labour
- Material
- Contractors' overheads and profit
- Scaffolding and plant required to carry out the work
- Value Added Tax.

For small items of work the costs have also included the contractors call out charge (see Page 10).

House Sizes
Where the cost is for work to a whole house, three examples are given to indicate the range of likely costs:
- Terraced. A terraced house of 21m^2 area on plan (42m^2 total on two floors).
- Semi-detached. A semi-detached house of 42m^2 area on plan (84m^2 total on two floors).
- Detached. This refers to a detached house of 125m^2 on plan (250m^2 on two floors).
  Elevation drawings of the houses used are included in Part Three.

Call out Charges
Contractors will often charge you for coming to your house. This is referred

to as a 'Call out charge'. For small items of work the call out charge may be more than the cost of carrying out the work. Some contractors will include the first half hour of any work in the call out charge, this is particularly common with 'emergency' services such as drain clearing.

Generally, call out charges have been included in items under £300.

BCIS carried out a survey of contractors' call out charges for this book. Call out charges differ between, and within, the trades. Call out charges for a general builder ranged from £20 to £90, plumbers £30 to £70, roofers £55 to £440 and electricians £25 to £95. The costs included in the rates given in the guide are:

*   General builder, carpenter, plumber, plasterer, glazier, painter   £60
*   Roofer   £220
*   Electrician   £45

Where more than one item of work is carried out on a single visit only one call out charge will apply and you should adjust the costs in the guide accordingly. An example of this adjustment is shown on Page 13.

Where a contractor has quoted for work the call out charges should be included in his quote.

The Cost Tables

Choosing the costs: The tables shows costs for items of works. Against each item, costs are given for a range of quantities.

In the example below, costs for hanging wallpaper are given for a wall of average height and various lengths. The area of wall is also given in m².

Description

Walls 2.75m high

Length	3m m² 8	4m m² 11	5m m² 14	8m m² 22
Repaper walls	**£**	**£**	**£**	**£**
Hang woodchip or embossed paper	185	225	265	385
Hang woodchip or embossed paper and decorate	260	330	400	530
Hang vinyl paper (PC £9 per roll)	275	370	435	575

Using the Costs from the Tables

Adjusting for quantity. The costs given are for a range of quantities eg. in the above example, for 8, 11, 14 and 22m2 of wall. You may need to adjust these for different quantities. This can be done in two ways.

Applying a unit rate. You can calculate a unit rate cost/m2 in this example and apply it to the required quantity.
Eg. Hanging 25m2 of woodchip paper:

$$22m^2 \text{ costs: } £385$$
$$1m^2 \text{ costs: } \frac{£385}{22} = £18/m^2$$
$$\textbf{25m}^2 \textbf{ costs: } £18/m^2 \times 25/m^2 = £450$$

Note that if you do the same calculation using the cost of 14m² this estimates the cost of hanging

25m² of woodchip paper at £475.

Pro-ratering. Alternatively, for some items where the range of costs is large you may wish to pro rata the costs between the quantities.
Eg. Hanging 10m² of woodchip paper:

11m² costs:	£225	
8m² costs:	£185	
3 additional m² costs:	£225-£185	
		=£40
1 additional m² costs:	$\frac{£40}{3}$	= £13
2 additional m² costs:	£13 x 2	= £26

10m²costs: £185+26   = £211
If the quantity of work is beyond the scope of the quantities given in a table an estimate can be made, within reason, by extrapolation. For example:
Eg. Hanging 25m² of woodchip paper:

22m² costs:	£385	
14m² costs:	£265	
8 additional m² costs:	£385-£265=£120	
1 additional m² costs:	$\frac{£120}{8}$	= £15
3 additional m² costs:	£15 x 3	= £45
25m² costs:	**£385+45 = £430**	

Adjusting for Location
The cost of building work varies around the country.

The costs in this guide represent UK 'national average costs'. They may need to be adjusted for location, and adjustment factors are provided in Section 3.3.

- If the total cost of the project is less than £1,000 then it is probably not worth adjusting for location.
- For projects likely to cost more than £1,000 it would be worth your thinking about the affect of location.

Using the Location Factors
The costs from the tables should be multiplied by the factors for the area where the project is located:

For example, costs in Wales are generally lower than the national average. The location factor for Wales is 0.96. Therefore, a project calculated to cost £100,000 from the table, is likely to cost £100,000 x 0.96 if it is located in Wales = £96,000.

Similarly, it is generally more expensive to build in Greater London. The location factor for London is 1.14. Therefore, a project calculated to cost £100,000 from the table, is likely to cost £100,000 x 1.14 if it is located in London = £114,000.

These adjustment factors relate to the cost of doing work and not the specification of the work. So adjusting the cost of installing a bathroom to London prices allows for the additional cost of fitting out a bathroom of a given standard, it does not allow for the difference in specification that might be appropriate in the different locations eg. between a B+Q bathroom and a Czech & Speake bathroom.

The location factors also allow comparison of costs between regions. If you know the cost of replacing a bathroom in Wales then you can work out what it might cost in London, as follows:

Known cost of our bathroom in Wales	**=£10,000**
Location factor for Wales	= 0.96
Location factor for Greater London	= 1.14
Difference in price between Wales and Greater London	$= \frac{1.14}{0.96} = 1.19$

Estimated cost of our bathroom in Greater London   = £10,000 x 1.19 = **£11,900**

Rounding

The costs in the tables have been rounded to reflect the nature of the guide. Generally costs have been rounded as follows:

- Less than £100 rounded up to the nearest £1 eg. £51.49 has been shown as £52.
- From £100 to £1000 rounded up to the nearest £5 eg. £846 has been shown as £850.
- Greater than £1000 rounded up to the nearest £10 eg. £1447 has been shown as £1450.

These rounding conventions are not intended to imply a level of predictive accuracy.

Cost Base and Inflation

The costs in the tables are current at 4th quarter 2007. Adjustments for future inflation can be found in Part Three, where forecasts of costs over the next three years are shown.

Costing Assumptions and Procurement Context

Costs in this guide are for completing the work described as an individual job. They include contractors' overheads, scaffolding, where applicable, and VAT. They exclude any temporary works, contingencies and any fees that may be applicable. Details of these items are described in Part Three.

Building costs are influenced by a range of factors such as:

- Quantity of work
- Quality of work
- When work is carried out
- Availability of space to work and store materials
- Provision of water and power
- The need for scaffolding
- Availability of materials and labour

These factors are the context in which you procure the work.

The costs in this guide are based on the assumptions about the procurement context that are given in the Costing Assumption in Part Three together with advice on how they influence costs. You should be aware of these assumptions and adjust the costs where actual circumstances differ.

There is no 'right' cost for building work. It is always an agreed price between a willing seller - the contractor, and a willing buyer - you. When there are shortages of labour prices will rise, when there is a shortage of work they will go down. In recent years, there has been a shortage of labour, an acute shortage in some areas, but the influx of builders from the new EU member states has helped to ease that situation.

The costs in this guide are intended to be reasonable where there is a sufficient supply of labour.

Costing Repairs – Examples
Example A

Property – 4 bedroom detached house. Gutter to front elevation is overflowing and two gutter joints are leaking due to blockage.

From Part 2 - Repairs - Exterior
Page 46
Clean out gutters
and outlets   £195

Page 46
Apply mastic sealant to
2 No. gutter joints   £91
                                        £287

Omit contractor's
callout charge   £-60
(The two charges included above
therefore reduce to one charge)
Total Cost of Works   **£226**
                            say   **£250**

Example B
Property – 3 bedroom semi detached
house. Insulation to roof space is
100mm thick and in very poor condition.

From Part 2.1 - Repairs - Insulation
Page 74
Clear out insulation, vacuum roof space
and lay 250mm thick glass fibre
insulation. Area of roof space
                                        58m²
Range:
Semi-detached House 42m² roof area
                                        £1285
Detached House 125m² roof area £3820

Unit cost £1285 ÷ 42 =   £31/m²
Cost of example
58m² @ £31/m² =   £1798
Total Cost of Works   **£1798**
                            say   **£1800**

Example C
Property: Any
Refurbish room size 3 x 3m on first
floor, replace two rotten floor joists and
badly damaged ceiling; redecorate
throughout and replace skirting and
carpet.

Replace joists and ceiling
From Part 2.1 Repairs
Page 79
Replace 50 x 150mm floor joist
Take up floor boards,
renew joists, refix boards
      3m long joists 2 No @ £210   £420

From Part 2.3 Finishes
Page 132
Replace ceiling
Replace plasterboard ceiling
and emulsion paint
      Room 3 x 3m 1 No @ £455   £455

From Part 2.4 Redecorations
Page 150
Clean and redecorate door and
frame (without fanlight) one side
      1 No @ £130   £130
Page 155
Clean and decorate window,
with two panes,
size 1500 x 1200mm
      1 No @ £95   £95
Page 148
Redecorate plaster walls
with emulsion paint to room 3m x 3m
                                     £310

From Part 2.3 Finishes
Page 134
Replace and decorate skirting
      Room 3 x 3m 1 No @ £340   £340
Page 133
Replace carpet and underlay   £740
                                  £2,490
Omit contractor's call out charge
(Four charges included above, remove
all as no call out charge required)
builder's call out charge
      4 No @ £60   £-240

Total Cost of Works   **£2250**
                      say   **£2300**

1.3 EMPLOYING A CONTRACTOR

When do I use a Contractor?
If you are not a DIY person then you will want to employ a contractor for everything. Even if you are DIY person there are some tasks that it will be prudent to ask a general builder or specialist tradesman to undertake.

Note: Most electrical and all gas work is required to be carried out by a suitably qualified tradesman.

It will always be more economical to 'bundle' work together so if there are several items of repair that need to be done, and you can afford it, then these can be included together into one contract.

When should I Consult a Surveyor or Engineer?
For most items of repair and redecorations, contractors can offer all the advice on specification that you will need. However, on larger projects or where there are major structural works or a high level of design is required, you should consider using the services of a surveyor, engineer or architect.

Finding a Surveyor, Engineer or Architect
There are again several ways of finding a local surveyor, architect or engineer although the best method is to contact the various Institutions, such as The Royal Institution of Chartered Surveyors, The Royal Institute of British Architects, and The Institution of Structural Engineers. The details of these organisations are to be found in Part Three.

Finding a Contractor
A Contractor may be found from a variety of sources:
- Word of mouth from family, friends and neighbours.
- Nameboards outside other properties where work is in progress.
- Contacting the Local Authority.
- Contacting local architects and surveying practices.
- Contacting the Federation of Master Builders to obtain a list of local contractors.
- Advertisements in local newspapers.
- Yellow Pages and Thomsons' telephone directories.
- Internet search.

Selecting a Contractor
It is absolutely essential that you get the right contractor to carry out the work.

Selection of the appropriate contractor/tradesman

Choose a contractor who has experience of doing the type of work that you need doing. If only one type of work is required, then it may be better to select a tradesman, such as a plumber, rather than a general builder.

For example, employ a roofer for roof work rather than a general contractor

If several different types of work are needed then it is usually correct to select the trade whose work makes up the largest proportion of the whole, however, some trades may not be prepared to act as main contractor.

For example:
Replacing a bathroom suite – select a plumber.

Refurbishing a bathroom complete with new suite, tiles, flooring, shelving, cupboards, lighting and redecoration – select a general builder who can supervise all trades he cannot undertake.

Choosing a contractor

You must select the contractor very carefully. While there may be a very large number of local builders, be as selective as possible in order to prevent any future problems both with the works and finances. The larger the project the more important this becomes.

In your search for a contractor, BCIS recommends the following sequence:

- Family and friends - Obtain recommendations from family and friends, in the area, who have had similar work undertaken.
- Recommendation - Speak to neighbours to ascertain if a contractor has been recommended by word of mouth.
- Nameboards – when driving around the area look for nameboards on properties where work is being carried out.
- Local Authority - contact the local planning/building inspection department and ask if they have a list of recommended contractors.
- Local architects/local surveyors - contact to see if they can recommend any companies.
- Letting Agencies – will usually rely on a small group of contractors to carry out repair work at tenancies they manage. They may be prepared to share their contacts with you.
- Builders Federations - Contact your local builders' association and ask for a list of registered members. The National Federation of Builders has 14 offices around the country, which can provide lists of registered builders in your area. This can similarly be undertaken

for specific tradesmen eg. electricians.

When several names have been collected, contact the companies and ask if you:

- Can inspect current/past work. (**Visit** the work, inspect the quality and speak to owners about the performance and standards of the contractor)
- Obtain references. (**Check** the references)
- Does the builder belong to a respected trade body? (**Call** body to confirm membership is current)

Discuss with the contractors/tradesman the work to be undertaken and confirm with them whether and when they will be able to carry out the works.

Where the works are of a substantial nature, the choice of a contractor may be limited to the larger size contractors in the area. Discussions with the contractor and examination of his present and immediate past schemes will reveal his suitability to the works required.

Large contractors sometimes have small works departments who are capable of carrying out minor repairs, however these may charge more as they will have higher overheads (office staff etc) than those of a small builder.

Preparing a Budget for the Works

When putting together a budget for larger projects, it is important that the budget is an estimate of the cost of the work, not an estimate of how much you have to spend.

Once you have prepared the budget for the work, you need to decide if you can afford it. This is particularly important if you are acting as a developer. Too many first time investors in property see the budget as the remainder of sale price less the cost of the property, selling and buying costs and desired profit.

A proper budget sets the price you are prepared to pay for the property, not the budget for the required building work.

For example:

Potential sale price of property when renovated		£350,000
Buying and selling costs	£20,000	
Required building work	£75,000	
Finance charges	£27,000	
Required profit	£30,000	
Other costs	£5,000	
	=	£157,000

Value of property to developer   **£193,000**

The budget should itemise all the required work and allow a contingency for unforeseen costs. The size of the contingency will depend on how sure you are of what you want and the level of alterations work that may uncover requirements for further work.

A contingency of 5% may be appropriate for a fully designed new extension, while 20% may be more appropriate if you are making major alterations to an old property.

Remember, this is your contingency budget, not the builders!

Estimates and Quotations

Before seeking estimates, make sure that you gather together as much information about the work as possible.

Select the appropriate materials. The cheapest are not necessarily the best, especially with regards to duration and future replacement.

Obtain information from manufacturers/installers as they will advise on the appropriate solution to a problem.

Allow a sum (possibly 10%) for contingency for hidden work or extra work that may arise during the contract. Builders may discover things that need fixing as jobs progress.

Obtain three quotes from contractors/tradesmen including the date that they will be able to commence the work. Ensure that the cost quoted will be fixed to the date they can undertake the work.

Request breakdowns of the quotes to examine and compare prices. A breakdown will also be extremely useful should variations and additional works be needed.

Contracts

A simple contract is a written **offer** to carry out the works for an amount and a written **acceptance** of that offer.

A simple but clear contract should be prepared for small contractors. However, for large contractors a formal contract using the Joint Contracts Tribunal (JCT) Minor Works Contract may be more appropriate.

Items that should be incorporated into a contract using small contractors/tradesmen should include:

- The cost of the work detailed on the drawing(s)/specification.
- The period of time the work is to be carried out in.
- Client requirements such as the contractor's access to the working area, any limitations on storage of

his materials and plant, and any protection required for other areas of the property during the execution of the works.
- The percentage of retention to be held by the client, and at what stage it will be released.
- The payment periods and calculation.
- Space for signature and dating by both parties.

Whilst the JCT contract is far safer both for the client and the contractor, for small builders this may be too onerous and they may be reluctant to price work that includes such a contract. Where the works are of a substantial nature, the employment of a professional surveyor, architect etc, is recommended. They will recommend the form of contract to use and prepare the documentation

Payments

On small contracts, where work may be expected to be completed in a few days, you should agree to pay the contractor on completion. Cash flow is always a problem for small businesses, and builders are no exception, so once you are happy with the work, but only when you are happy, pay promptly.

Never pay in advance. It is almost impossible to recover money overpaid without recourse to expensive legal action. If a contractor asks for payment for materials, agree either to pay the supplier directly or on delivery.

On larger projects the payment periods and calculation should be specified in the contract.

For example:
'Valuations shall take place on a fortnightly basis and shall be valued on the work completed by that date. Payment shall be made to the contractor within seven days of the valuation.'

Do not pay early for work and especially, do not overpay early.

Include the adjustment for retention with each payment

The calculation of how much is owing to a contractor is called a 'Valuation'.

An example of a valuation is set out as follows;

Value of total scheme including variations £53,000

Valuation No. 3

Value of work undertaken to date	£36,000
Variations No.1 and 2 completed	£2,000
Total of work completed	£38,000
Less retention @ 5%	£1,900
Total less retention	£36,100
Less Valuations 1 and 2	**£28,400**
Total	**£7,700**
Value Added Tax @ 17.5%	£1,348

Total due to contractor – Valuation No.3   **£9,048**

On completion of the works, carry out an inspection with the contractor and agree where any items have not been finished.

For example:
A new door is fitted including new ironmongery and decoration but the door does not close and on inspection requires planing on one side and subsequently redecorating.

Once the works have been fully completed, the retention can then be released.

Retention

This is a sum of money set aside by the client [you] from the contract sum until the works are completed to your satisfaction.

The inclusion of retention gives you some financial leverage and safeguard should some items of work, albeit minor, not be completed to your satisfaction. The money withheld will not be released until all the works are completed satisfactorily.

Should the contractor leave the site and not return to complete the outstanding works, you will have funds available to

have the work completed by others. You should notify the contractor if you are going to do this.

The details of the retention requirement should be set out in the original contract. It is usual to express retention as a percentage of the cost of the work, 5% being an appropriate and usual percentage.

Any variations should be included in the adjustment for retention.

As the works progress and payments are made, so the retention should be included with the payment calculations, see example under payments.

Variations and Extras

Always try to avoid changing your mind about what you want. However, even on the best run schemes 'stuff' happens, so changes are required.

Always obtain prices before agreeing for additional works to be undertaken, and confirm the work and cost in writing. Consult with the contractor as early as possible on possible variations, and ensure variations do not arise on work that has already been completed.

It may be a good idea to include additional works to an existing contract, rather than carry out this work at a later date as a separate job.

For example:
Existing job – replacing bathroom suite, retiling two walls to half room height, redecorating room.

Additional work; tile all walls to full height.

If the tiling hasn't commenced and the tiles are readily available then it should be cheaper and will be less disruptive if the work is added into this contract.

Keep variations and extra work to a minimum. If there are too many variations or even one variation of large importance/size then this may have an adverse effect on the contract completion date and therefore could increase costs.

When contracts of repair and refurbishment are undertaken, extra work may arise from hidden unforeseen problems.

For example:
Existing job – replacing ceiling.
On removal of the ceiling, the joists are found to be rotten and require replacing.

It may be prudent to allow a larger contingency sum in the budget for such works, to cover for any unforeseen or additional works.

1.4 PLANNING AND BUILDING LEGISLATION AND REGULATIONS

Introduction

If you are altering or extending your property there are two kinds of approval that you may require from your local authority.

- Planning permission – this is approval to increase the amount of building, so relates generally to extensions or outbuildings.

- Building Regulations – this is approval that building work is being carried out in accordance with the current Building Regulations. It relates to all new work and all structural alterations.

- It should be noted that the information given in this section on planning permission and building regulations relates to Enland and Wales. Planning Permission requirements and building regulations may differ slightly in Scotland and Northern Ireland. In any case, always check requirements with your local authority before carrying out any work.

Planning Permission

Planning permission is the responsibility of the Local Authority.

It is permission to erect or extend a building.

Before commencing work on the design, it is generally a good idea to contact the Local Authority planning officer to seek their requirements and advice. The level of informal advice that you get depends very much on the individual planning officer.

For formal planning permission, the Authority will normally charge a fee. You [the applicant] will be required to submit your application using forms obtainable from the Authority.

Should you do the work without the necessary approvals, the Local Authority can issue an enforcement notice. This notice might require that you seek retrospective planning permission approval. However, there is no guarantee that retrospective permission will be granted. The Local Authority may even require that the completed work be demolished.

Listed buildings and properties in a conservation area have special planning requirements. Similarly, flats also have special planning requirements. It is again recommended that the Local Authority planning officer is consulted as early as possible on these types of properties.

Extensions

Planning permission for a single or two storey structure will depend on the floor area/volume in relation to the existing property.

Planning permission is required:
- In England and Wales, if the total addition to the original house is more than 70m^3 or 15% of the volume of the original house, up to a maximum of 115m^3, whichever is the greater. For a terraced house or property in a conservation area this is 50m^3 or 10%. In Scotland, if the total addition to the original house is more than 50m3 or one fifth of the volume of the original house, up to 115m3, whichever is the greater. If the house has been extended before, this must be added to the new work and together this must be less than the limit.
- When the extension is within 20m of the highway. If, however, the original house is less than 20m from the highway, the proposed extension must not be nearer to the highway than the original house.
- Any part of any extension, within 2m of the boundary, is more than 4m high.
- The extension projects above the highest part of the original house.
- The total area of the extension exceeds half of the garden area.

Note: Measurements are taken around the outside of the house.

Conservatories

The rules for conservatories will be the same as for single storey structures, above.

Porches

Planning permission is required for porches if:

- The floor area exceeds 3m2.
- Part of the porch is higher than 3m above ground.
- Part of the porch is less than 2m from the boundary between the garden and the public footpath/road.

Garages and car ports

If the garage is located within 5m of the original building, it will be considered as an extension and the same rules apply.

If the garage is situated more than 5m from the original building, planning permission is required if:

- The floor area is more than 15m^2.
- The height is more than 3m high for a flat roof or 4m high for a pitched roof.
- There is sleeping accommodation.
- The garage covers more than half the area of the garden (excluding the area covered by the house).
- Part is less than 1m from a boundary.
- Part projects beyond any wall of the property facing the road.
- Use is only for anyone other than the house occupants.

Loft conversions

Loft conversions are subject to the same rules as extensions.

The volume to be considered will be only the additional volume outside the existing roof, eg. the volume created if a new dormer window is to be installed. In most cases, therefore, the increase in volume will be small.

Walls, fences and gates

Planning permission is required if walls, fences and gates are higher than 2m, or if they adjoin a highway they must be higher than 1m.

Building Regulations

Building Regulation approval is the responsibility of the Local Authority.

These Regulations define how the new building is to be constructed and ensure that the building is structurally safe, and that:

- New or existing foundations are adequate for the new construction.
- Rainwater and drainage conform to requirements.
- Staircases etc meet safety requirements.
- Ventilation, thermal insulation and fire safety regulations are complied with.

It is recommended that, before commencing work on the design, you contact the Local Authority building control officer to seek their requirements and advice.

The Authority will normally charge a fee and the applicant will be required to submit his application using forms obtainable from the Authority. A fee will also be charged for the visits by the building inspector.

The local building inspector will visit the site at specified stages in its construction in order to inspect the work. The building inspector may change requirements following his inspection, if he deems them necessary. For example, one of his first inspections will be carried out after the foundation

trenches have been excavated. He will be in a position to examine the subsoil, and if not of a requisite standard, he could instruct that the depth of foundation be increased before the concrete is poured.

Structural alterations to existing building

All structural alterations such as forming openings, removing walls, removing chimney breasts etc, require Building Regulation approval. If you are not sure what is and what is not structural, consult the Local Authority, a surveyor or engineer.

Single or two storey structures built onto the existing building

Building Regulations approval is required where the extensions contain habitable rooms.

Conservatories

The definition of a conservatory is a building, which is attached to a building. It has more than 75% of the roof areas and more than 50% of the wall areas as translucent materials.

Building Regulations approval is required:
- When floor area exceeds 30m².
- When the conservatory is classified as a habitable room.

Porches
Building Regulations approval is required:
- When floor area exceeds 30m2.

Garages and car ports
Building Regulations approval is required:
- If the garage adjoins the house.
- If the garage is detached, and
  - When floor area exceeds 30m².
  - It is not more than 1 metre from a boundary or
  - It is more than single storey height, and
  - It is not constructed wholly of non-combustible material.
  - There is sleeping accommodation.
- If the car port is:
  - Not open on at least two sides, and
  - When floor area exceeds 30m².

Loft conversions
Building Regulations approval is required.

The structural requirements for any extension will apply here. The existing loft may create problems with regards to both headroom and the size of the existing floor joists.

If the loft is created on a third or higher floor then there must be an adequate means of fire escape. Possible solutions include:
- Enclosing the stairway and landing with a minimum 30 minutes fire resisting material.

- Access through a window and external ladder.

Walls, fences and gates
Building Regulations approval is required:
- If the walls, fences and gates are higher than 2m.
- If the walls, fences and gates adjoining a highway are higher than 1m.

All electrical work
Part P (Electrical Safety) of the Building Regulations now requires all electrical work to be carried out by certified people except very limited work.

Work that can be carried out by non-certified operatives:
- Replacement of light fittings, sockets, switches.
- Replacement of damaged cable for a single circuit.
- Work not in the bathroom and kitchen comprising;
  - Additional lighting, fittings and switches to existing circuit.
  - Additional sockets and fused spurs to existing ring or radial main.
  - Additional earth bonding.

These works are conditional upon:
- The use of suitable cable and fittings for the particular application.
- Circuit protective measures are unaffected and suitable for protecting the new circuit.
- All works comply with all other appropriate regulations.

Work that must be carried out by certified operatives:

- All new modifications to electrical wiring within bathrooms and shower rooms.
- Installation or modification to underfloor heating.
- Installation or modification to ceiling heating.
- Power or lighting to garden.
- Specialist installations.

Replacement windows and doors

Building Regulations approval is required for replacement windows and doors. The Government operates a Competent Persons Scheme for replacement windows and doors, which means that approved installers can self certify that their work is carried out in accordance with current Building Regulations, and consequently, you do not need to apply for local authority building control approval. Currently, approved schemes are operated by FENSA (www.fensa.co.uk) and CERTASS (www.certass.co.uk), and if your installer is approved by one of these schemes, local authority building control approval should not be required. It is recommended, however, to check that your local authority recognises FENSA or CERTASS.

DIY work

Building Regulations will apply equally to DIY work and work undertaken by a contractor. The Local Authority will need to be notified of DIY changes before the work is commenced. The work will be inspected and tested.

Certificates

You will need to keep the appropriate certificates from the Local Authority to prove that any work was approved. You will need to produce them when you come to sell the house.

Competent Persons Self Certification Schemes

These schemes are approved by the Government, and allow certain work to be carried out by approved contractors, who self certify that their work is carried out in accordance with the current Building Regulations. The contractors are vetted by approved organisations, who ensure members have the appropriate and relevant levels of competence to carry out the work. Once the work is complete, the contractor should either issue a certificate to the consumer to the effect that the work is in accordance with current Building Regulations, or inform the scheme organisers who will in turn issue a certificate. The schemes avoid the consumer having to apply to the local authority for prior building control

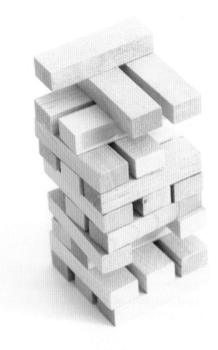

approval, but it is recommended to check that your local authority recognises the approved scheme organisers. Further information on Competent Persons Schemes, the type of work covered, and approved organisers can be found at: www.communities.gov.uk/planningand building/buildingregulations/competent personsschemes/.

Asbestos removal

The disposal of asbestos is strictly regulated. You should contact your local council for advise on removal of items containing asbestos, such as asbestos ceiling tiles and board partitioning, asbestos cement sheets and tiles, asbestos lagging or asbestos lined fire doors. If you need a licenced asbestos removal contractor, you can find your nearest on the Asbestos Removal Contractors' Association website (www.arcaweb.org.uk).

Party Walls

If the property is a terraced or semi detached house then a wall (or walls if a mid terrace) will be shared with a neighbour. This shared wall is known as the party wall.

You must obtain your neighbours consent before any of the following building work is started:
- Extensions
- Structural alterations
- Some internal refurbishment
- Damp proofing works

In some cases, if excavations or constructing foundations for a new construction are within 3m or 6m of the neighbouring property, then written consent will also be required.
Your neighbour cannot in normal circumstances withhold consent, as long as the provisions of the Party Wall etc Act are followed.

The Party Wall etc. Act 1996

The Party Wall etc. Act 1996 produced a procedure for homeowners in England and Wales. It applies to all building work involving a party wall or party fence wall. The Act was designed to minimise disputes by ensuring property owners use a surveyor to determine the time and way in which the work is carried out.

An 'agreed surveyor' can be used to act for both owners should problems arise.

The Act covers the following and written agreement is required:
- Bearing of beam – cutting into wall for eg. a loft conversion or supporting upper floor after removal of a loadbearing internal wall.
- Damp proof course – inserting new all the way through the wall.
- Underpinning the party wall.
- Demolishing and rebuilding the party wall.
- Raising the whole party wall including cutting off any objects, if necessary preventing this from happening.
- Protecting adjoining walls by cutting a flashing into an adjoining building.
- Building a new wall on the line of the junction between two properties.
- Excavating foundations:
- Within 3m of an adjoining structure and lower than its foundation.
- Within 6m of an adjoining structure and below a line drawn down 45 degrees from the bottom of its foundation.

The Act does not cover the following and written agreement is not required:
- Minor works not affecting the neighbour's part of the party wall.
- Fixing plugs.
- Fixing skirting or other woodwork.
- Screwing in wall units.
- Screwing in shelving.
- Replastering walls.
- Adding or replacing electrical wiring or socket outlet.

Notice of party wall work
Written notice must be given to neighbours:
- **At least two months** before starting any party wall works.
- **One month** for building a wall between properties or excavation works.

If tenants or leaseholders live next door, the landlord must also be informed. Written notice must also be given to owners living above or below the property.
Endeavour to talk to neighbours before issuing notices as this can prevent any future problems.

Neighbours should give written approval within 14 days of receipt of the notice.

Disputes
If there is a dispute:
- Both parties appoint their own surveyor or
- Both parties appoint 'agreed surveyor'.

The surveyor will draw up the 'Award', a document which details work to be carried out, when and how it is to be done, and a record of the condition of the adjoining property before the work is started.

The Award will determine who will pay for the work if this is in dispute, although this is generally the property owner who started the work.

Party wall guidance
A useful guide, 'Party Wall Guidance' can be obtained free of charge from the Royal Institution of Chartered Surveyors. It provides information on party wall law and where you can go for advice. Visit: www.rics.org/partywalls.

Building Materials
The selection of buildings materials will be dependent upon the existing property, especially the external fabric. Another factor is how close it is to other buildings and how they are constructed. These factors affect the materials and design, particularly the front elevation/elevation facing the main road.

Building materials do have a bearing both when obtaining Planning, and Building Regulations approval. It is again recommended that you discuss selection before going ahead.

Where possible, and especially on the elevation facing the main road, the materials chosen for the external fabric such as bricks, roof tiles, windows, doors, should match or be sympathetic with the existing property.

Grants

There are a number of grants available to householders, some of which are listed below. They are obtained from Local Authorities and the householder is therefore recommended to contact them to discuss whether the work they envisage qualifies for a grant, what proportion of the cost may be given by the Authority, and the rules governing the award of a grant.

The law sets out a framework of all the various work that is eligible for a grant, however each authority may have their particular guidelines to determine what work has funding priority.

Renovation grants

This grant is discretionary and will be available for either large-scale works to make a house fit for habitation, or to put a house into reasonable repair.

These grants may be available if the house is in serious disrepair, deemed unfit to live in, and the owner cannot afford to pay for these repairs.

The types of work, which would be considered for a grant, are:

- Installing a fixed bath or shower, wash basin, sink, including hot and cold water supply, and an inside toilet, where none previously existed in the building.
- Extensive dampness.
- Any work which has been instructed by the Local Authority, under a statutory notice or order:
  - If the property is in a serious state of disrepair.
  - If the property does not meet with their standards under law, eg no inside toilet.
  - If the property is in a Housing Action Area.
  - If the house is occupied by more than one family and a fire escape may be required.

Grant assistance is not available for routine repair and maintenance work, eg. repainting front door, renewing tap washer.

Authorities can award grants for work costing up to £20,000 in total. The grant will be set at 50% of the cost up to the £20,000 maximum.

Empty homes grants

These may be available from an authority and they are given to enable an empty property to be brought back into a habitable condition.

The grant available will vary with each authority, but will typically range from, £1000 or 50% of the cost of eligible works, up to a maximum of £5000 per habitable room.

Authorities may differ on their rules regarding the interpretation of 'empty', eg. a property has been empty for at least six months, a property has been unoccupied and no Council Tax has been paid for three months or more.

Disabled facilities grants

These are available for the adaptation of a property to meet the recommended disabled occupants health needs, eg. enlarging a separate toilet to enable wheelchair access and the fitting of grab rails.

Lead pipe replacement

Small grants may be separately available towards the replacement of lead supply pipes.

Insulation grants

These may be available to cover the cost of works to improve the thermal insulation of a property.

Home Information Packs (HIPs)

As from 14 December 2007, all properties marketed for sale in England and Wales require Home Information Packs (HIPs). These HIPs include important information about the property, and include both compulsory and non compulsory information. It is important to remember, that when you have work carried out to your property which requires planning permission, building regulations approval and other certificates, you are likely to have to include evidence of these in a Home Information Pack.

One of the compulsory documents is an Energy Performance Certificate which states how energy efficient a home is on a scale of A – G. Those properties rated A are the most efficient homes, and should have lower fuel bills.

More information on HIPS can be found on the Home Information Pack's web site at:
www.homeinformationpacks.gov.uk

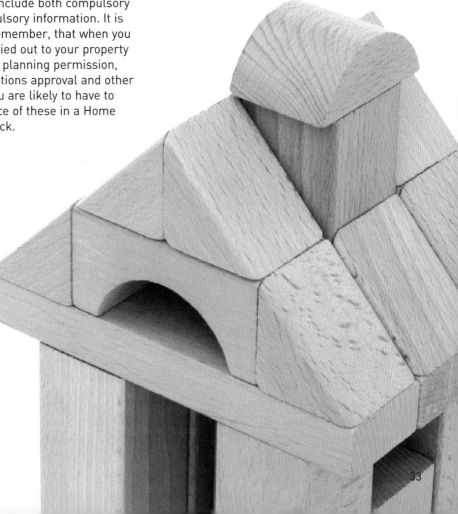

1.5 MAJOR PROPERTY PROBLEMS

When looking at a property it is important to consider the factors that may have contributed to problems as well as the problems themselves. In some circumstances, treating the symptoms not the disease can lead to problems reoccurring.

The causes of major property problems can be classified as follows:
- Original construction.
- Maintenance of building – poor maintenance of building once construction has been completed.
- Maintenance around building.
- Movement.
- Weather conditions.
- Finance.

Original Construction

Throughout the years there have been times when either labour and/or materials shortages, or the urgency to put up buildings while demand was strong, has lead to sub-standard construction and the use of sub-standard materials.

World wars and natural disasters also contribute, from time to time, in altering the standards of labour and materials.

For example:
Poor quality or undersized softwood used in the original construction can lead to the timber deteriorating. Initial poor preparation and decoration may further contribute to timber decay. This results in the need to repair or replace much earlier than might be expected.

Maintenance of the Building

Lack of maintenance can lead to major maintenance problems.

If repairs are not carried out when the problem first arises, other areas of the property can be affected thus exacerbating the problem.

For example:
A blocked gutter, if not cleared quickly, can cause the gutter joints and gutter itself to break. Water overflowing can cause dampness to penetrate the building. Staining to brickwork, whilst not a major problem, can become unsightly. Continued damp penetration will lead to wood rot in any timber in contact with the wall.

For example:
A lack of redecoration to external joinery, particularly where paint has fallen off or joints have shrunk, can cause problems with rot to the woodwork.

Maintenance around the Building

Problems can occur from the following:

Trees, shrubs:
- Root action can cause ground shrinkage, pressure in foundations and damage drains.
- Removal of a large tree can alter the ground conditions, causing below ground water problems and subsequently movement to the building.
- Trees and shrubs close to the building can cause damp to penetrate through the external fabric.
- Falling leaves block gutters and gullies. A build up against the external wall of the building can cause damp to penetrate through the external fabric.

- Structural damage - a large tree falling onto the building can cause structural damage. Large branches breaking off can also cause damage to the roof tiling etc.

Creepers: Climbing plants such as ivy
- Mortar failure between bricks in external walls.
- Damage to the face of brickwork.
- Damage to vertical boarding, fascias, rainwater gutters, roof tiling/slating including battens and felt, ie. anywhere that the creeper can grow between or into.
- Block outlets such as flues, extract and gas ventilators.

Ground level above dpc:
- Soil is allowed to bank up above the damp proof course (dpc), leading to damp penetration of solid walls.
- A footpath is constructed along the external wall at, or above, the height of the damp proof course.

Maintenance audit
The Royal Institution of Chartered Surveyors (RICS) recommends that house-owners carry out regular checks of their properties to ensure early detection of potential problems.

Subsidence
The RICS recommends that house-owners check their properties for signs of subsidence. Subsidence, which is caused by the loss of water from shrinkable subsoil, brought about by a period of high temperatures and low rainfall, is a major threat to houses built with shallow foundations. Houses built pre-1965 tend to have shallow foundations which are more susceptible to the seasonal changes in the top metre of soil.

Regular checks should be made of the property for any cracks that appear. Cracks over 15 -25mm wide are considered to be 'severe' and require action, especially if they pass through brickwork or stone. On finding a crack, householders should immediately notify their insurance company, or their landlord.

Autumn
The RICS advises house-owners to carry out a regular autumn maintenance check of their properties. The checks and solutions listed below may prevent a small job turning in to a much bigger one.

Autumn maintenance checks and solutions are:
- **Roof**
  - o   Inspect the roof and replace any cracked tiles.
  - o   If chimney pots are in place but not in use consider protecting them, by fitting ventilated cowls.

- **Loft**
  - Check the insulation is in good condition.
  - It is important that the tanks and pipes in the loft do not freeze, so do not insulate below the tank and insulate any pipes above the loft insulation
  - Make sure the lid is on the cold-water tank.
- **Gutters/drains**
  - Clear them of leaves and debris. Take particular care that the gulleys are clear.
  - Overflowing gutters can drench walls and cause damage.
- **Walls**
  - Around a third of heat lost in the home is through the walls. Cavity wall insulation is a good option.
  - Check the pointing – frost can play havoc with poorly maintained walls.
  - Make sure water can run off the building; fill gaps to cement angle fillets at wall junctions.
- **External paving**
  - In very cold weather water on paving will freeze.
  - Ensure the paving is well drained and avoid water collecting, freezing and causing accidents.
- **Decking**
  - Check that it hasn't obstructed air bricks and gulleys.
- **Windows**
  - Check perimeters of all windows to make sure water flows away from glass and doesn't collect on the sill, or drain behind it.
  - It is important to minimize drafts. If double-glazing is not in place (which can cut the cost of heat loss through windows by around a half), consider fitting cheaper options such as secondary glazing or put polythene across the window frames.
  - Curtains can make a big difference to heat loss.
- **Doors**
  - Stop draughts through letterboxes by fitting a cover and put a sealant around the door frames.
- **Floor boards**
  - If there are stripped floors in place, consider putting down rugs in the winter to reduce up drafts between the boards.
- **Heating systems**
  - Check your heating system is in order; service boilers, insulate hot water tanks, bleed radiators.

While many of these simple tasks can be undertaken safely in the home, it is important that people seek the advice of reputable professional plumbers and builders when looking to complete larger jobs.

Movement

Movement of the structure of a building can be caused by the building moving or the ground moving, either of which can create major structural problems and can be caused by:

- Inadequate foundations.
- Proximity of large trees.
- Adverse weather conditions.
- Changes to local ground conditions, eg by removal of large tree, changes to paving and/or hardstandings.

- Traffic - particularly applicable to older houses built along main roads and due to the increase in traffic in recent years, especially heavy goods lorries.

Weather Conditions

Adverse weather conditions such as heavy rain or periods of drought, can affect the structure of the ground and consequently movement damage can follow.

High winds can weaken parts of the structure such as roof tiling/slating, chimneys.

Rates for items likely to be damaged due to storm, flood, snow and earthquake are now included in section 2.7.

Finance

It may have occurred that, at the time a repair was necessary, funds were not available. A repair may then have been carried out using an inferior or inappropriate material and/or cheaper less skilled labour. This may have been deemed a temporary measure at the time, however, if the repair is not corrected at a later date then increased problems may arise.

For example:
The use of hard mortar or render to replace original lime mortar in old properties can lead to cracking to brickwork or damp retention behind the render.

PART TWO

2:1 REPAIRS

EXTERIOR
Replace Roof Coverings

	Tiles/slates in One Location (m²)			
	1 £	2 £	5 £	6 £

AREAS OF TILES/SLATES MISSING OR BROKEN ON ROOF

SOLUTION
Replace missing/broken tiles/slates

	1	2	5	6
Plain clay tile	355	455	485	590
Concrete interlocking tile	305	355	495	545
Natural slate	420	580	795	955

	Tiles/slates in One Location (number)			
	1 £	2 £	5 £	6 £

INDIVIDUAL OR SEVERAL TILES/ SLATES MISSING OR BROKEN ON ROOF

SOLUTION
Replace missing/broken tiles/slates

	1	2	5	6
Plain clay tile	285	305	325	330
Concrete interlocking tile	285	305	325	330
Natural slate	290	315	340	350

INDIVIDUAL OR SEVERAL TILES/ SLATES LOOSE ON ROOF

SOLUTION

	1	2	5	6
Resecure tiles/slates	280	290	305	310

	Area (m²)		
	10 £	15 £	25 £

FELT TO FLAT ROOF IS LEAKING

Inspection recommends replacement

SOLUTION

Replace three layer felt roof	650	860	1280

FELT TO FLAT ROOF IS LEAKING AND BOARDING IS DAMAGED

Inspection recommends replacement

SOLUTION

Replace three layer felt roof and boarding	865	1300	2170

FELT TO FLAT ROOF IS LEAKING, BOARDING AND INSULATION IS DAMAGED

Inspection recommends replacement

SOLUTION

Replace three layer felt roof, boarding and insulation	1810	2700	4480

ASPHALT TO FLAT ROOF IS LEAKING

Inspection recommends replacement

SOLUTION

Hack up asphalt roofing and apply 19mm two coat work on felt and underlay.	650	1010	1730

FELT TO FLAT ROOF IS LEAKING

Inspection recommends replacement

SOLUTION

Prepare existing mastic asphalt and overlay with HP felt	575	760	1130
Apply one coat bituminous paint	315	365	465
Apply two coats bituminous paint	570	745	1100

	Repairs (number)		
	1 £	2 £	5 £

SMALL PATCHES IN TOP LAYER OF FELT ROOF ARE DAMAGED OR SPLIT

SOLUTION
Cut out defective layer, rebonding to adjacent layers and covering with single layer felt

	1 £	2 £	5 £
Small patches not exceeding 0.5m^2	250	280	370
0.5 - 2m^2	265	310	445
2 - 5m^2	315	410	695

SMALL DEPRESSIONS HAVE APPEARED IN ROOF DECK

SOLUTION

	1 £	2 £	5 £
Repair felt and boarding	285	340	530

AREA OF FELT ROOF IS DEVOID OF CHIPPINGS

SOLUTION
Clear stone chippings, dress surface with compound and recover with chippings

	1 £	2 £	5 £
Small patches not exceeding 0.5m^2	250	280	355
0.5 - 2m^2	255	280	375
2 - 5m^2	280	340	525

BLISTERS OR CRACKS IN ASPHALT

SOLUTION

	1 £	2 £	5 £
Cut out detached blister and make good, 0.5m^2 area	250	275	345
Cut out crack and make good, per m run	255	285	375

ROOF LEAKING AT JUNCTION OF WALL AND ROOF

Inspection recommends replacement of lead flashing

SOLUTION

	Length of Flashing (m)			
	1 £	2 £	5 £	6 £
Replace flashing up to 225mm girth	420	495	570	645
Replace stepped flashing up to 240mm girth	555	665	770	880
Parapet box gutter 650mm girth including boxed end, cover flashing, dress into rainwater head	1660	2080	2510	2900
Valley gutter 600mm wide	2120	2610	3100	3600

DAMP PATCH INTERNALLY AT TOP OF CHIMNEY BREAST

SOLUTION

Replace chimney flashing

	Length (mm)	
	700 £	1200 £
Replace back gutter to chimney stack, 500mm girth	405	455

ROOF FLASHING IS CRACKED OR LOOSE

SOLUTION

Repair flashing.

	Length of Crack (m)			
	4 £	5 £	6 £	7 £
Repair crack in sheeting, clean out and fill with solder	235	260	285	315
Refix existing lead flashings with new wedges and repoint with mortar	305	350	395	440

	Repairs (number)			
	1 £	2 £	3 £	5 £
Repair crack not exceeding 150mm long and fill with solder	130	140	150	175
Repair crack not exceeding 150 to 300mm long and fill with solder	140	155	170	190

	RANGE House Type		
	Terraced	Semi-Detached	Detached
	£	£	£

EAVES OR VERGE BOARDING IS LOOSE

SOLUTION

Resecure eaves fascia, including decoration

	Terraced	Semi-Detached	Detached
ONE ELEVATION	230	280	420
WHOLE HOUSE	395	720	1310

Resecure eaves soffit, including decoration

	Terraced	Semi-Detached	Detached
ONE ELEVATION	240	290	445
WHOLE HOUSE	420	760	1390

Resecure eaves fascia and soffit, including decoration

	Terraced	Semi-Detached	Detached
ONE ELEVATION	335	430	725
WHOLE HOUSE	605	1130	2290

Resecure verge boarding, including decoration
One Side Elevation

	Terraced	Semi-Detached	Detached
ONE SIDE	280	255	350
BOTH SIDES	455	405	595

	Length of Gutter/Pipe (m)		
	1	2	3
	£	£	£

GUTTERS ARE MISSING OR DAMAGED

SOLUTION
Replace gutters

PVCu	140	180	215
Aluminium	155	205	265
Cast iron, including decoration	190	280	370

RAINWATER DOWN PIPES ARE MISSING OR DAMAGED

SOLUTION
Replace pipes

PVCu	130	160	190
Aluminium	160	215	270
Cast iron, including decoration	205	305	405

	Fittings (number)		
	1	2	3
	£	£	£

RAINWATER FITTINGS ARE MISSING OR DAMAGED

SOLUTION
Replace head/hopper

Cast aluminium, powder coated finish	130	190	250
Fabricated aluminium, powder coated finish	190	315	440
Cast iron, including decoration	115	165	215

Replace shoes

PVCu	94	120	145
Aluminium	110	155	200
Cast iron	115	160	205

Replace balloon grating

PVCu	71	79	87

Replace gutter brackets

PVCu	71	79	87
Galvanised repair bracket	79	94	110

GUTTER JOINTS ARE LEAKING

SOLUTION
Repair joints

	Fittings (number)		
	1	2	3
	£	£	£
Apply mastic sealant to gutter joint	**77**	**91**	**105**

GUTTERS ARE OVERFLOWING

SOLUTION
Clean out or realign gutters and downpipes

		RANGE House Type		
		Terraced	Semi-Detached	Detached
		£	£	£
Clean out gutters, outlets etc				
	ONE ELEVATION	**135**	**145**	**195**
	WHOLE HOUSE	**205**	**300**	**580**
Realign gutters PVCu				
	ONE ELEVATION	**250**	**310**	**510**
	WHOLE HOUSE	**430**	**740**	**1590**
Metal				
	ONE ELEVATION	**300**	**375**	**625**
	WHOLE HOUSE	**530**	**915**	**1970**
Realign down pipes PVCu				
	ONE ELEVATION	**240**	**240**	**265**
	TWO ELEVATIONS	**420**	**420**	**335**
Metal				
	ONE ELEVATION	**290**	**290**	**325**
	TWO ELEVATIONS	**520**	**520**	**580**

	Pots per Stack	£	RANGE	£

CHIMNEY STACK IN POOR CONDITION, LEANING
Inspection recommends rebuilding

SOLUTION
Rebuild stack 1m high, reset existing pots

	1	**2080**	to	**2570**
	2	**2570**	to	**3560**
	4	**3750**	to	**4540**

Rebuild stack 1m high, replace 450mm high pots

	1	**2170**	to	**2760**
	2	**2970**	to	**3750**
	4	**4340**	to	**5130**

Rebuild stack 1m high, replace 900mm high pots

	1	**2370**	to	**2970**
	2	**3360**	to	**4150**
	4	**5130**	to	**5930**

Rebuild stack 2m high, reset existing pots

	1	**2760**	to	**3560**
	2	**4150**	to	**5130**
	4	**4540**	to	**5720**

Rebuild stack 2m high, replace 450mm high pots

	1	**2970**	to	**3750**
	2	**4340**	to	**5520**
	4	**5130**	to	**6520**

Rebuild stack 2m high, replace 900mm high pots

	1	**3150**	to	**3950**
	2	**4740**	to	**5930**
	4	**5930**	to	**7300**

POINTING TO CHIMNEY STACK IN POOR CONDITION

SOLUTION
Repoint 1m high stack

	1	**715**	to	**770**
	2	**750**	to	**835**
	4	**770**	to	**890**

Repoint 2m high stack

	1	**810**	to	**950**
	2	**890**	to	**1070**
	4	**945**	to	**1190**

EXTERIOR
Repoint Flashings and Replace pots to Chimney Stacks

		Pots per Stack		
		1	2	4
		£	£	£

POINTING TO CHIMNEY STACK
FLASHINGS IN POOR CONDITION

SOLUTION
Repoint flashings at base of chimney stack

		1	2	4
Front or back flashing	ONE SIDE	**205**	**205**	**210**
Stepped flashing	ONE SIDE	**215**	**260**	**260**
All flashings around chimney	ALL SIDES	**285**	**330**	**340**

CHIMNEY POTS DAMAGED OR MISSING

SOLUTION
Replace pots and flaunching

	1	2	4
450mm high pot	**760**	**930**	**1270**
900mm high pot	**960**	**1330**	**2070**

Single
Items
£

TV AERIAL IS LOOSE

SOLUTION
Refix aerial to chimney stack, including renewing fixings   **215**

EXTERNAL WALLS REQUIRE REBUILDING

SOLUTION
Rebuild external skin of cavity wall

	ELEVATION	Terraced	RANGE House Type Semi-Detached	Detached
		£	£	£
Rebuild wall	FRONT OR REAR	**7120**	**16820**	**25870**
Rebuild wall including new wall insulation batts	FRONT OR REAR	**7780**	**18220**	**27910**
Rebuild wall including replacing polystyrene insulation	FRONT OR REAR	**7870**	**18440**	**28240**

		End Terrace Semi- Detached		Detached
		£		£
Rebuild wall	SIDE	**23410**	to	**24980**
Rebuild wall including new wall insulation batts	SIDE	**25570**	to	**26960**
Rebuild wall including replacing polystyrene insulation	SIDE	**25890**	to	**27260**

EXTERNAL BRICK WALLS REQUIRE REPOINTING

		Terraced	RANGE House Type Semi-Detached	Detached
		£	£	£

SOLUTION
Repoint external wall

		Terraced	Semi-Detached	Detached
Repoint external wall	ONE ELEVATION	**790**	**1340**	**2190**
	WHOLE HOUSE	**1570**	**4260**	**7590**

DAMP IS PENETRATING THROUGH EXTERNAL WALL

There is no existing damp course or the damp course has failed

SOLUTION
Install hessian based damp proof course

		Terraced	Semi-Detached	Detached
	ONE ELEVATION	**330**	**500**	**1050**
	WHOLE HOUSE	**670**	**1350**	**3320**

Inject silicone damp proofing

		Terraced	Semi-Detached	Detached
	ONE ELEVATION	**190**	**330**	**515**
	WHOLE HOUSE	**300**	**660**	**1630**

		RANGE		
		House Type		
	ELEVATION	Terraced	Semi-Detached	Detached
		£	£	£

EXTERNAL BRICK WALLS ARE DIRTY/STAINED

SOLUTION
Spray with water and brush lightly

		Terraced	Semi-Detached	Detached
	ONE ELEVATION	845	1480	2380
	WHOLE HOUSE	1690	5180	9230
Sandblast				
	ONE ELEVATION	1080	1970	3110
	WHOLE HOUSE	2150	6970	12060

		RANGE		
		Quality of Bricks		
		£		£

BRICK FACES ARE DAMAGED OR CRACKED

Area of Patch (m²)

SOLUTION
Replace defective bricks at low level

(no scaffolding required)

Area of Patch (m²)	£		£
1	215	to	320
2	320	to	520
3	470	to	785
5	775	to	1310

Replace defective bricks at high level

(scaffolding required)

1	240	to	340
2	340	to	540
3	510	to	825
5	820	to	1350

BRICKWORK HAS CRACK

Length of Crack (m)

SOLUTION
Cut out brickwork and replace with new brickwork at low level

(no scaffolding required)

1	135	to	190
2	210	to	325
3	290	to	450
5	445	to	650

Cut out brickwork and replace with new brickwork at high level

(scaffolding required)

1	155	to	230
2	240	to	380
3	335	to	490
5	490	to	700

Crack in Brickwork

Crack in Pointing

INDIVIDUAL BRICKS ARE DAMAGED OR CRACKED

	Bricks (number)	RANGE Quality of Bricks		
		£		£

SOLUTION
Replace defective bricks at low level

Bricks (number)	£		£
1	64	to	75
2	75	to	80
5	98	to	115
10	140	to	175

Replace defective bricks at high level

Bricks (number)	£		£
1	85	to	94
2	94	to	100
5	120	to	140
10	165	to	200

HOLES IN BRICKWORK AFTER PIPES HAVE BEEN REMOVED

SOLUTION
Fill holes

	Holes (number)			
	1	2	3	5
	£	£	£	£
Half brick thick walls	90	100	110	130
One brick thick walls	95	110	125	155

POINTING TO BRICK WALLS IN POOR CONDITION

SOLUTION
Rake out joints and repoint

	RANGE House Type		
	Terraced	Semi-Detached	Detached
	£	£	£
ONE ELEVATION	785	2240	3510
WHOLE HOUSE	1570	7980	13670

POINTING TO SMALL AREAS OF
BRICK WALLS IN POOR CONDITION

SOLUTION
Repoint

	Area of Patch (m²)			
	1	2	3	5
	£	£	£	£
Pointing at low level				
Rake out joints and repoint by machine	130	175	220	310
Rake out joints and repoint by hand	135	190	245	355
Pointing at high level				
Rake out joints and repoint by machine	155	205	250	340
Rake out joints and repoint by hand	165	220	280	395

CRACK HAS APPEARED ALONG
POINTING IN BRICKWORK

SOLUTION
Repoint crack in joint

	Length of Crack (m)			
	1	2	3	5
	£	£	£	£
Pointing at low level				
Cut out crack and repoint to match existing	86	95	105	145
Pointing at high level				
Cut out crack and repoint to match existing	115	130	145	175

	Length of Pointing (m)			
	1	2	3	5
	£	£	£	£

**POINTING HAS BECOME LOOSE
ALONG FLASHING**

SOLUTION
Repoint mortar along flashing

	1	2	3	5
Pointing at low level				
Rake out joint and point in flashing	89	100	115	145
Pointing at high level				
Rake out joint and point in flashing	125	135	145	165

**POINTING HAS BECOME LOOSE
AROUND DOOR OR WINDOW FRAMES**

SOLUTION
Repoint around frames

	1	2	3	5
Pointing at low level				
Rake out joint and repoint in mortar or mastic	90	110	125	155
Pointing at high level				
Rake out joint and repoint in mortar or mastic	125	140	155	185

**CRACKS AROUND LINTELS,
INSUFFICIENT BEARING OR LINTEL
HAS FAILED**

	RANGE Size Variation		
	£		£
SOLUTION			
Replace lintel at low level			
Replace concrete lintel	325	to	375
Replace steel lintel	345	to	475
Replace lintel at high level			
Replace concrete lintel	385	to	440
Replace steel lintel	415	to	535

	ELEVATION	RANGE House Type		
		Terraced £	Semi-Detached £	Detached £
EXTERNAL STONE WALLS REQUIRE REPOINTING				
SOLUTION				
Repoint stone walls, hard mortar	ONE ELEVATION	1500	2880	4440
	WHOLE HOUSE	2990	10290	17300
EXTERNAL STONE WALLS REQUIRE CLEANING				
SOLUTION				
Spray with water and brush lightly, plain wall	ONE ELEVATION	945	1690	2700
	WHOLE HOUSE	1890	5960	10450
Sandblast, plain wall	ONE ELEVATION	1180	2180	3420
	WHOLE HOUSE	2350	7730	13280
EXTERNAL RENDERING IS IN POOR CONDITION				
SOLUTION				
Rerender with two coats cement and sand render	ONE ELEVATION	1400	2670	4130
	WHOLE HOUSE	2790	9530	16080
EXTERNAL RENDERING DECORATION IS IN POOR CONDITION				
SOLUTION				
Prepare and apply one coat exterior cement paint	ONE ELEVATION	630	990	1670
	WHOLE HOUSE	1250	3400	6420
EXTERNAL RENDERING DECORATION IS BADLY STAINED				
SOLUTION				
Prepare and apply one coat fungicidal treatment	ONE ELEVATION	590	915	1570
	WHOLE HOUSE	1180	3140	6010
EXTERNAL PEBBLE DASH IS IN POOR CONDITION				
SOLUTION				
Replace pebbledash	ONE ELEVATION	1530	2960	4550
	WHOLE HOUSE	3060	10560	17710

RENDERING IS DAMAGED

	Small Patch n.e. 0.5m (number) £	Area (m²) 1 £	Area (m²) 2 £	Area (m²) 5 £
SOLUTION				
Repair rendering at low level				
Two coats cement and sand render, decorated	150	195	265	475
Repair rendering at high level				
Two coats cement and sand render, decorated	180	225	300	525

PEBBLE DASH IS DAMAGED

	Small Patch n.e. 0.5m (number) £	1 £	2 £	5 £
SOLUTION				
Repair pebbledash at low level				
Pebble dash finish	150	180	245	435
Repair pebbledash at high level				
Pebble dash finish	185	215	280	475

BRICKWORK IS STAINED

	Area (m²) 1 £	2 £	5 £	10 £
SOLUTION				
Cleaning at low level				
Sandblasting	98	140	260	460
Spraying with water	85	115	200	340
Cleaning at high level				
Sandblasting	125	170	335	610
Spraying with water	110	140	245	425

	Individual Board (number) £	Area (m²)		
		2 £	3 £	5 £

VERTICAL SHIPLAP CLADDING IS DAMAGED

SOLUTION

Replace cladding at low level

Replace softwood boarding	120	320	430	650
Replace pvc cladding	100	245	330	500

Replace cladding at high level

Replace softwood boarding	155	345	460	690
Replace pvc cladding	165	285	370	540

	Area (m²)			
	2 £	3 £	5 £	6 £

VERTICAL TILING IS MISSING OR DAMAGED

SOLUTION

Replace tiles or slates at low level

Replace vertical tiles	310	425	650	765
Replace vertical slates	475	720	1210	1460

Replace tiles or slates at high level

Replace vertical tiles	355	470	700	815
Replace vertical slates	520	765	1260	1500

	Tiles in One Location (number)		
	1 £	5 £	10 £

Replace tiles or slates at low level

Replace vertical tiles	125	180	245
Replace vertical slates	130	200	285

Replace tiles or slates at high level

Replace vertical tiles	160	215	280
Replace vertical slates	165	235	325

	RANGE	
	Quality of Material	
	£	£

EXTERNAL DOOR IS DAMAGED

SOLUTION
Replace doors and frames as necessary

Replace external door
Remove door, hang new door including refixing ironmongery
and decoration to both sides | **405** to | **630**
Remove door, hang new door including new ironmongery
and decoration to both sides | **580** to | **950**

Replace doors and frames
Replace timber door and frame with PVCu
door and frame | **930** to | **1130**

EXTERNAL DOOR IRONMONGERY IS NOT FUNCTIONING

SOLUTION
Replace external door ironmongery

	£		£
Renew rim lock and SAA lever furniture	**88**	to	**120**
Renew steel butts, one and half pairs	**110**	to	**155**
Renew mortice deadlock	**110**	to	**180**
Renew cylinder mortice latch	**185**	to	**295**
Renew letter plate	**115**	to	**130**

GLASS TO DOOR IS BROKEN OR CRACKED

SOLUTION
Hack out broken glass and putty and reglaze single door

	£		£
One pane size 150 x 150mm in half glazed panel door	**68**	to	**69**
All panes size 150 x 150mm in half glazed panel door	**95**	to	**130**
Half glazed panel door	**100**	to	**125**
Fully glazed panel door	**160**	to	**210**

	Single Items £

PUTTY IS MISSING OR DAMAGED

SOLUTION
Replace putty

One pane size 150 x 150mm in half glazed panel door	**63**
All panes size 150 x 150mm in half glazed panel door	**96**
Half glazed panel door	**66**
Fully glazed panel door	**69**

GLAZING BEADS ARE MISSING OR DAMAGED

SOLUTION
Replace glazing beads including decoration

One pane size 150 x 150mm in half glazed panel door	**74**
All panes size 150 x 150mm in half glazed panel door	**235**
Half glazed panel door	**85**
Fully glazed panel door	**105**

	Single Items £

DOORS AND FRAMES DAMAGED OR NOT CLOSING, THRESHOLDS UNSATISFACTORY

SOLUTION
Repair doors and frames

Ease door without removal	**68**
Take down door, ease, adjust and rehang	**82**
Take down door, shave 12mm from bottom edge and rehang	**82**
Remove door, shave sides and top and bottom edges to fit opening, rehang	**115**

Ease and adjust doors and frames

Ease and adjust door and frame of any size, adjust door stops, refix architraveand frame, overhaul ironmongery and leave in good working order	**110**

Repair/replace door frames and thresholds

Take off door and rehang, remove and refix ironmongery as necessary, make good decorations and leave in good working order

Repair single door and frame of any size	**160**
Replace softwood door frame	**320**
Replace hardwood threshold	**250**

Replace water bar

Galvanised steel bar bedded in mastic, to single door opening	**125**

Repoint one side with polysulphide sealant

Single door frame	**82**
Threshold	**66**

Insert external threshold seal with weather board strip

Single door opening	**110**
Single door opening to doors with water bar	**155**

	RANGE	
	Approx Window Size (mm)	
	600 x 900	1200 x 1200
	£	£
WINDOW IS DAMAGED OR ROTTEN		
SOLUTION		
Replace window at low level		
Take out and install new double glazed window		
PVCu casement window	270 to	690
PVCu sash window	1040 to	1930
Take out and install new double glazed window including decorating externally		
Timber casement window	545 to	770
Timber sash window	815 to	1300
Metal casement window	625 to	825
Replace window at high level		
Take out and install new double glazed window		
PVCu casement window	340 to	760
PVCu sash window	1110 to	1990
Take out and install new double glazed window including decorating externally		
Timber casement window	610 to	845
Timber sash window	880 to	1370
Metal casement window	690 to	895

	Approx Window Size (mm)	Single Items £
WINDOW IS DAMAGED OR ROTTEN		
SOLUTION		
Replace window at low level		
Take out and install new double glazed window		
PVCu casement window	1800 x 1800	**1550**
PVCu sash window	1800 x 1800	**4340**
Take out and install new double glazed window including decorating externally		
Timber casement window	1800 x 1800	**1740**
Timber sash window	1800 x 1800	**2910**
Metal casement window	1800 x 1800	**1860**
Replace window at high level		
Take out and install new double glazed window		
PVCu casement window	1500 x 1200	**970**
PVCu sash window	1500 x 1200	**2520**
Take out and install new double glazed window including decorating externally		
Timber casement window	1500 x 1200	**1070**
Timber sash window	1500 x 1200	**1720**
Metal casement window	1500 x 1200	**1140**
OPENING WINDOW IS STICKING		
SOLUTION		
Ease opening casement or sash without removal		**68**
Renew sash cord to single sash		**105**
Renew both sets of sash cords to single window		**115**
SECONDARY GLAZING UNIT DOES NOT OPERATE		
SOLUTION		
Remove and refit unit, of any size		**73**

Single
Items
£

OPENING WINDOWS AND IRONMONGERY STICKING, PUTTY AND BEADS ROTTEN OR MISSING

SOLUTION
Ease and adjust casement or sash window, overhaul ironmongery, renew
beads with putty and sprigs, adjust stops and beads   **110**

WINDOW IN POOR CONDITION

SOLUTION
Piece in damaged area of frame, sill or casement with new timber, renew
broken glass as necessary, overhaul or provide new ironmongery   **195**

WINDOW SILL IS ROTTEN

SOLUTION
Cut out sill complete and replace, including decoration
600mm long   **185**
1800mm long   **330**

POINTING AROUND WINDOW FRAME IS MISSING OR LOOSE

SOLUTION
Repoint frame, up to window size 1800 x 1800mm   **90**
Repoint window sills 600 - 1800mm long   **68**

SEALS AROUND SASH WINDOWS ARE MISSING OR DAMAGED

SOLUTION
Install seal to window size 650 x 1050   **210**
Install seal to window size 900 x 1200   **250**

IRONMONGERY TO WINDOW IS MISSING OR INOPERABLE

SOLUTION
Renew casement stay and fastener   **85**
Renew sash fastener   **81**
Renew cast iron sash weight   **120**

| | RANGE | |
| | Approx Pane Size (mm) | |
	300 x 600 £	900 x 900 £
WINDOW PANE IS BROKEN		
SOLUTION		
Remove glass and putty, prepare and reglaze	**110** to	**230**
PUTTY AROUND PANE IS MISSING OR LOOSE		
SOLUTION		
Replace putty	**69** to	**75**
PROBLEM		
Glazing beads around pane are missing or damaged		
SOLUTION		
Replace glazing beads including decoration	**96** to	**130**

	Canopy Area 750mm x		
	1200mm £	1950mm £	3000mm £

ENTRANCE CANOPY IS DAMAGED

SOLUTION
Replace canopy

	1200mm	1950mm	3000mm
Softwood framed canopy with roof tiles on plywood	615	990	1580
GRP canopy with tile effect roof	400	515	790

	RANGE	
	£	£

MAJOR CRACKS AND/OR BOWING IN EXTERNAL WALL

SOLUTION

Structural report recommended	**900**	to	**1200**

Report states that foundations of property should be underpinned

		RANGE	
		House Type	
	Terraced	Semi-Detached	Detached
	£	£	£

UNDERPIN

Underpin including removing and later reinstating soil

	Terraced	Semi-Detached	Detached
ONE WALL	**2450**	**3650**	**7250**
WHOLE HOUSE	**4900**	**9700**	**23000**

Underpin including breaking up and later reinstating concrete paving

	Terraced	Semi-Detached	Detached
ONE WALL	**2650**	**3950**	**7850**
WHOLE HOUSE	**5200**	**10400**	**24800**

MINOR CRACKS IN EXTERNAL WALLS

SOLUTION
Replace damaged bricks to external wall

Replace, at low level

	Area of brickwork m^2		
Area of brickwork	1	**215**	to	**320**
	2	**320**	to	**520**
	3	**470**	to	**785**
	5	**770**	to	**1310**

	Length of crack m		
Length of crack	1	**135**	to	**190**
	2	**210**	to	**325**
	3	**290**	to	**450**
	5	**450**	to	**665**

	Individual bricks number		
Individual bricks	1	**64**	to	**74**
	2	**74**	to	**79**
	5	**100**	to	**110**
	10	**140**	to	**160**

RANGE
Quality of Bricks

£   £

MINOR CRACKS IN EXTERNAL WALLS

SOLUTION

Replace damaged bricks to external wall

Replace, at high level

	Area of Brickwork m²			
Area of brickwork	1	**240**	to	**340**
	2	**340**	to	**540**
	3	**510**	to	**825**
	5	**820**	to	**1350**

	Length of Crack m			
Length of crack	1	**155**	to	**230**
	2	**240**	to	**380**
	3	**335**	to	**490**
	5	**490**	to	**700**

	Individual Bricks number			
Individual bricks	1	**85**	to	**94**
	2	**94**	to	**105**
	5	**120**	to	**135**
	10	**165**	to	**185**

DAMP PENETRATING WALL AT LOW LEVEL
Ground level is above the existing damp proof
course (dpc)

SOLUTION
Excavate as necessary to ensure that finished
ground level is a minimum 150mm below the
existing damp proof level, remove soil and
consolidate, to a minimum width of one metre

		RANGE		
		House Type		
		Terraced	Semi-Detached	Detached
		£	£	£
Excavate soil only				
	ONE WALL	175	225	375
	WHOLE HOUSE	230	510	1250
Excavate soil and lay new gravel path				
	ONE WALL	195	260	445
	WHOLE HOUSE	280	600	1460
Excavate soil and lay precast concrete paving slabs				
	ONE WALL	370	515	890
	WHOLE HOUSE	625	1280	2810
Excavate soil and lay 100mm thick concrete path, with formwork to edge, to falls, tamped finish				
	ONE WALL	450	640	1140
	WHOLE HOUSE	785	1560	3600

	Length (m)			
	1	2	3	5
	£	£	£	£
Excavate soil only	97	125	150	200
Excavate soil and lay new gravel path	105	135	170	230
Excavate soil and lay precast concrete paving slabs	145	220	295	445
Excavate soil and lay 100mm thick concrete path, with formwork to edge, to falls, tamped finish	170	260	360	560

DAMP PENETRATING WALL AT LOW LEVEL
No damp proof course in wall

SOLUTION
Cut out two courses of brickwork and insert hessian damp proof course, pointing in mortar and making good brickwork or inject silicone damp proofing

	RANGE		
	House Type		
	Terraced	Semi-Detached	Detached
	£	£	£
Install hessian based bitumen damp proof course			
ONE WALL	330	500	1050
WHOLE HOUSE	670	1350	3320
Inject silicone damp proofing			
ONE WALL	190	330	515
WHOLE HOUSE	300	660	1630

DAMP PENETRATING SOLID EXTERNAL WALL AND PLASTER

SOLUTION
Apply one coat exterior waterproof compound to brickwork, concrete, rendered surfaces

	Area (m^2)			
	1	2	3	5
	£	£	£	£
One coat exterior waterproof compound	83	95	110	135

DAMP PENETRATING PLASTER/WALL OF CAVITY WALL

SOLUTION
Clean out blocked cavities from outside, include cutting out facing bricks, clearing mortar droppings and renewing bricks to match existing

	Number of Locations			
	1	2	3	5
	£	£	£	£
Clean out cavities by removing three bricks	130	185	240	350

**DAMP PENETRATION THROUGH
WALLS AT VARIOUS LOCATIONS,
AROUND WINDOWS AND DOORS,
AT CEILING HEIGHT**

SOLUTION
Insert damp proof course

	Length (m)			
	1 £	2 £	3 £	5 £
Work to cavity walls at low level				
Cut out one course of bricks in any quality facing bricks, in short lengths (approximately 675mm) and insert polypropylene refurbishment cavity tray, renew facings to match existing	150	230	305	460
Cut out one stepped course bricks, any quality facing bricks, and insert combined cavity dpc preformed polypropylene and lead cavity tray, renew bricks to match existing	240	310	495	825
Take off copings, prepare wall, insert damp proof course and relay coping	130	180	230	330
Work to cavity walls at high level				
Cut out one course of bricks in any quality facing bricks, in short lengths (approximately 675mm) and insert polypropylene refurbishment cavity tray, renew facings to match existing	175	255	335	495
Cut out one stepped course bricks, any quality facing bricks, and insert combined cavity dpc preformed polypropylene and lead cavity tray, renew bricks to match existing	265	340	525	875
Take off copings, prepare wall, insert damp proof course and relay coping	150	205	255	365

INTERNAL WALLS ARE DAMP

SOLUTION
Hack off existing plaster, rake out joints in
brickwork/blockwork for key, apply three coat
asphalt tanking, cement and sand render and refix
or install new skirting to match existing, decorate
wall

	RANGE		
	House Type		
	Terraced	Semi-Detached	Detached
	£	£	£
Asphalt tanking to 1.2m high (decorate full height)			
ONE WALL	**1400**	**2090**	**4170**
WHOLE HOUSE	**2790**	**5560**	**13190**
Asphalt tanking to full height of ground floor wall			
ONE WALL	**2910**	**4350**	**8700**
WHOLE HOUSE	**5810**	**11600**	**27540**

	Floors to Room		
	Room Size		
	3 x 3m	4 x 4m	8 x 4m
	£	£	£
Asphalt tanking to 1.2m high (decorate full height)	**3060**	**4460**	**6130**
Asphalt tanking to full height of ground floor wall	**7810**	**10700**	**17280**

GROUND FLOORS ARE DAMP

SOLUTION
Remove flooring, screed and skirting from
room, lay 500 gauge bitumen coated
polyethylene membrane and priming, or two
coat asphalt tanking, reinstate screed and refix
skirting

		RANGE		
			House Type	
		Terraced	Semi-Detached	Detached
		£	£	£
Bitumen coated polyethylene membrane	WHOLE HOUSE	**1900**	**3810**	**11320**
Mastic asphalt tanking	WHOLE HOUSE	**2280**	**4570**	**13570**

		RANGE		
		Bitumen		Mastic Asphalt
		£		£
	Room Size			
Lay tanking and reinstate screed only				
	3 x 3 m	**820**	to	**980**
	4 x 4m	**1460**	to	**1740**
	8 x 4m	**2910**	to	**3480**
Lay tanking, reinstate screed and lay new flooring				
	3 x 3 m	**1510**	to	**2040**
	4 x 4m	**2680**	to	**3620**
	8 x 4m	**5360**	to	**7240**

WALLS TO KITCHEN OR BATHROOM ARE DAMP

SOLUTION
Install extract fan in external wall, including
forming hole through cavity, or glass to window

	RANGE	
	Quality of Fan	
	£	£
Install extract fan	**285** to	**460**

INSULATION IN ROOF AREA IS DAMAGED OR MISSING

SOLUTION
Clear out insulation, vacuum roof space and lay 250mm thick glass fibre insulation

RANGE		
House Type		
Terraced	Semi-Detached	Detached
£	£	£
640	**1285**	**3820**

Length (m)			
1	2	3	5
£	£	£	£
92	**125**	**155**	**215**

INSUFFICIENT THICKNESS OF INSULATION
250mm thick is recommended

SOLUTION
Lay 150mm thick glass fibre insulation over existing insulation

RANGE		
House Type		
Terraced	Semi-Detached	Detached
£	£	£
425	**720**	**2150**

Length (m)			
1	2	3	5
£	£	£	£
78	**95**	**110**	**140**

DIFFICULTY WITH ACCESS ACROSS
ROOF SPACE

SOLUTION
Install 1m wide timber flooring as walkways

Length of Walkway (m)	RANGE		
	Plywood £		Softwood £
1	**89**	to	**180**
2	**120**	to	**260**
3	**150**	to	**355**
5	**205**	to	**490**

	RANGE		
	House Type		
	Terraced £	Semi-Detached £	Detached £

IMPROVE INSULATION LEVEL TO
EXTERNAL WALLS

SOLUTION
Inject cavity wall with foam or mineral fibre system

	Terraced	Semi-Detached	Detached
	440	**1510**	**2400**

IMPROVE INSULATION LEVEL TO
PANELLED EXTERNAL WALLS

SOLUTION
Hack off render, replace or install new insulation panel with rigid insulation board and metal lathing and rerender to match existing

	Terraced	Semi-Detached	Detached
ONE WALL	**4160**	**8750**	**12950**
WHOLE HOUSE	**8310**	**31730**	**50790**

As above but including one coat exterior stone paint to render

	Terraced	Semi-Detached	Detached
ONE WALL	**4400**	**9290**	**13710**
WHOLE HOUSE	**8790**	**33670**	**53790**

	Walls 2.75m High Length (m)			
	3 £	4 £	5 £	8 £

IMPROVE INSULATION LEVEL TO WALLS

SOLUTION

Take down plasterboard to internal skin, install insulation, fix new plasterboard, skim coat and decorate	455	625	795	1310
Construct plasterboard timber stud partition with insulation, plasterboard, skim coat, skirting and decoration to one side	1270	1750	2220	3640

WATER TANK INSULATION MISSING OR DAMAGED

SOLUTION

Replace insulating jacket

	RANGE Per Jacket		
	£		£
Replace insulating jacket around cold water tank	245	to	305
Replace insulating jacket around hot water cylinder	110	to	135

INSULATION TO PIPEWORK IS DAMAGED OR MISSING

SOLUTION

Replace insulation to pipework

	Length of Pipework(m)			
	1 £	2 £	5 £	10 £
Replace pipe insulation in roof space or cupboards	73	85	120	175
Replace pipe insulation to pipes under floors, pipes running in direction of floor boarding	79	98	150	235
Replace pipe insulation to pipes under floors, pipes running in opposite direction of floor boarding	120	175	330	590

INSUFFICIENT VENTILATION
IN ROOF SPACE

SOLUTION
Improve ventilation

	RANGE		
	House Type		
	Terraced	Semi-Detached	Detached
	£	£	£
Remove tile or slate from roof slope and install tile vents	255	595	1515
Form hole in boarding at eaves and install ventilator at 1m centres			
ONE ELEVATION	120	135	205
TWO ELEVATIONS	180	205	305
Form hole in boarding at eaves and install continuous plastic ventilator			
ONE ELEVATION	155	185	305
TWO ELEVATIONS	240	305	505
Remove ridge tiles and install ridge vent at 2m centres, with adaptor, make good all work disturbed	275	400	1080

	Vents (number)			
	2	4	6	8
	£	£	£	£
Remove tile or slate from roof slope and install tile vents	425	610	820	945
Remove ridge tiles and install ridge vent at 2m centres, with adaptor, make good all work disturbed	690	1140	1390	1830

SECTION OF ROOF TIMBER IS DECAYED OR DAMAGED

SOLUTION
Cut out existing decayed, split etc. timber and splice in softwood treated timber

	Length of Timber (m)		
	1	2	3
	£	£	£
Rafters or purlins	**160**	**250**	**340**
Ridges	**165**	**270**	**375**

WHOLE OF ROOF TIMBERS ARE DECAYED OR DAMAGED

SOLUTION
Replace existing decayed, split etc. timber and splice in softwood treated timber

	Length of Timber (m)		
	4	5	6
	£	£	£
Rafters or purlins	**380**	**480**	**580**
Ridges	**425**	**525**	**625**

VENTILATE FLOORS TO PREVENT FUTURE DAMAGE TO TIMBER

SOLUTION
Ventilation is recommended to prevent further decay

Install louvred ventilator in internal wall and air brick in external wall
NOTE: air bricks should be located at 1.8m intervals along external walls

		RANGE Quality of Bricks		
		£		£
	Number of bricks			
Solid or cavity wall	1	**140**	to	**180**
	2	**205**	to	**290**
	3	**270**	to	**400**
	5	**345**	to	**550**

FLOOR JOISTS ARE ROTTEN OR SPLIT

SOLUTION
Replace Joist

Replace 50 x 150mm floor joist	Length of Timber (m)			
	1	2	3	5
	£	£	£	£
Take up floor boards, renew joist, refix boards	110	160	210	310
Take up flooring, renew joist, lay new softwood boarded flooring	190	315	435	675
Take up flooring, renew joist, lay new chipboard flooring	130	205	270	410
Replace 50 x 225mm floor joist				
Take up floor boards, renew joist, refix boards	125	185	245	365
Take up flooring, renew joist, lay new softwood boarded flooring	205	340	470	730
Take up flooring, renew joist, lay new chipboard flooring	140	230	310	470

TIMBER FLOOR IS TOO SPRINGY

SOLUTION
Install herringbone strutting

Install 50 x 30mm softwood herringbone strutting between existing joists	Lengths of Strutting (m)			
	1	2	3	5
	£	£	£	£
Take up floor boards, install strutting, refix boards	85	110	135	185
Take up flooring, renew joist, install strutting, lay new softwood boarded flooring	125	165	210	300
Take up flooring, renew joist, install strutting, lay new chipboard flooring	115	170	225	335

Install 100 x 50mm softwood solid strutting between existing joists				
Take up floor boards, renew joist, install strutting, refix boards	88	115	140	190
Take up flooring, renew joist, install strutting, lay new softwood boarded flooring	125	175	220	310
Take up flooring, renew joist, install strutting, lay new chipboard flooring	120	185	250	380

TIMBER FLOOR AND JOISTS ARE DECAYED
OR DAMAGED

SOLUTION
Take up flooring to expose joists, treatment as necessary,
refix or replace flooring, treat flooring and/or joists

		RANGE		
		House Type		
	Number	Terraced	Semi-Detached	Detached
	of Floors	£	£	£
Treat timber floor/joists				
Apply water repellant preservative				
To softwood flooring	Both floors	300	400	1030
	One floor	150	240	515
To softwood flooring and joists	Both floors	960	2120	6800
	One floor	480	1060	3400
Apply woodworm treatment				
To timber flooring	Both floors	330	445	1250
	One floor	165	270	625
To timber flooring and joists	Both floors	1070	2380	7560
	One floor	535	1190	3780
Replace timber flooring				
Softwood butt jointed boards	Both floors	2520	5640	17920
	One floor	1260	2820	8960
Softwood tongued and grooved boards	Both floors	2740	6120	19460
	One floor	1370	3060	9730
Chipboard flooring, butt jointed	Both floors	980	2180	6900
	One floor	490	1090	3450
Chipboard flooring, tongued and grooved joints	Both floors	1180	2640	8360
	One floor	590	1320	4180

TIMBER FLOOR AND JOISTS ARE DECAYED

SOLUTION
Take up flooring to expose joists, treatment as necessary

Treat timber floor/joists

	Floors to Room Room Size		
	3 x 3m £	4 x 4m £	8 x 4m £
Apply water repellant preservative			
To softwood flooring	120	150	215
To softwood flooring and joists	330	445	900
Apply woodworm treatment			
To timber flooring	125	160	250
To timber flooring and joists	355	500	1000

	Area of Flooring (m^2)			
	1 £	2 £	3 £	5 £
Apply water repellant preservative				
To softwood flooring	79	84	88	96
To softwood flooring and joists	105	135	160	215
Apply woodworm treatment				
To timber flooring	81	85	90	100
To timber flooring and joists	105	140	175	240

TIMBER FLOOR IS BADLY DAMAGED

SOLUTION
Take up and replace flooring

Replace timber flooring

	Floors to Room Room Size		
	3 x 3m	4 x 4m	8 x 4m
	£	£	£
Softwood butt jointed boards	665	1180	2360
Softwood tongued and grooved boards	730	1300	2600
Chipboard flooring, butt jointed	330	460	920
Chipboard flooring, tongued and grooved joints	390	555	1110

	Area of Flooring (m²)			
	1	2	3	5
	£	£	£	£
Softwood butt jointed boards	180	250	345	530
Softwood tongued and grooved boards	190	270	370	570
Chipboard flooring, butt jointed	120	150	185	255
Chipboard flooring, tongued and grooved joints	130	160	200	280
Hardboard, fixed with nails	93	110	130	165
Plywood fixed with nails	105	135	160	215

TIMBER JOISTS ARE DECAYED OR DAMAGED

SOLUTION
Take up flooring to expose joists, replace joists, refix or replace flooring

	Area of Flooring (m²)			
	1	2	3	5
	£	£	£	£
Take up floor boards, renew joist, refix boards				
Softwood butt jointed boards	125	165	215	310
Softwood tongued and grooved boards	130	175	220	315
Take up flooring, renew joist, lay new flooring				
Softwood butt jointed boards	190	315	425	580
Softwood tongued and grooved boards	205	330	455	635
Chipboard flooring, butt jointed	140	205	270	395
Chipboard flooring, tongued and grooved joints	150	215	285	425

FLOOR IS SCORED AND DIRTY

SOLUTION
Sand or cover floor to whole room

| | | RANGE | |
| | | House Type | |
	Terraced	Semi-Detached	Detached
	£	£	£
Clean and sand boarded floor			
GROUND FLOOR	595	1190	3540
FIRST FLOOR	485	1070	3420
WHOLE HOUSE	1080	2260	6960
Lay hardboard on existing timber floor			
GROUND FLOOR	390	770	2290
FIRST FLOOR	300	700	2210
WHOLE HOUSE	690	1470	4500
Lay plywood on existing timber floor			
GROUND FLOOR	605	1210	3580
FIRST FLOOR	490	1090	3470
WHOLE HOUSE	1095	2300	7050

| | Floors to Room | | |
| | Room Size | | |
	3 x 3m	4 x 4m	8 x 4m
	£	£	£
Sand or cover floor to whole room			
Clean and sand boarded floor	320	450	900
Lay hardboard to surface of existing timber floor, fix with nails	260	355	710
Lay plywood to surface of existing timber floor, fix with nails	320	460	920

**FLOOR BOARDS ARE LOOSE
AND UNEVEN**

SOLUTION
Lift and refix softwood floorboards

	RANGE		
	House Type		
	Terraced	Semi-Detached	Detached
	£	£	£
GROUND FLOOR	**385**	**880**	**2630**
FIRST FLOOR	**300**	**800**	**2540**
WHOLE HOUSE	**685**	**1680**	**5170**

	Floors to Room		
	Room Size		
	3 x 3m	4 x 4m	8 x 4m
	£	£	£
Softwood boarded flooring throughout room	**250**	**400**	**675**

	Area of Flooring (m²)			
	1	2	3	5
	£	£	£	£
Softwood boarded flooring, in small areas	**82**	**105**	**125**	**165**

	Height of Flue (m)			
	5 £	6 £	11 £	12 £

FLUE LINING MISSING

SOLUTION
Repair cracks

Line flue with concrete flue linings				
First floor flue	365	395	—	—
Ground floor flue	—	—	450	470

	Number of Chimneys	
	1 £	2 £

DAMP IS PENETRATING THROUGH
WALLS OF SEALED CHIMNEY STACK

SOLUTION
Cut opening in bricked up chimney breast, provide and fix
plaster louvre ventilator size 150 x 225mm | 95 | 135

CHIMNEY FLUE IS BLOCKED

SOLUTION
Sweep chimney | 62 | 90

	Single Items £

SEVERE CRACKING OVER FIREPLACE OPENING

SOLUTION

Replace lintol over opening, make good plaster and emulsion paint	**610**

MANTLE IS DAMAGED

SOLUTION

Replace pine mantle	**375**
Replace micro marble mantle	**920**

HEARTH IS DAMAGED

SOLUTION

Replace hearth with Decostone	**375**
Replace hearth with conglomerate marble	**440**

FIREPLACE IS DAMAGED

SOLUTION

Replace with conglomerate marble back panel and hearth, pine mantle	**705**
Replace with green marble or black granite back panel and hearth, stone micro marble mantle	**2350**

FIREBACK IS DAMAGED

SOLUTION

Replace fireback for solid fuel fire	**230**
Replace fireback for gas fire	**265**

	RANGE	
	Quality of Materials	
	£	£

INTERNAL DOOR IS DAMAGED OR MISSING

SOLUTION

Replace flush door, reuse existing ironmongery, decorate	**245**	to	**400**
Replace flush door, fix new ironmongery, decorate	**295**	to	**515**
Replace six panel door, reuse existing ironmongery, decorate	**445**	to	**735**
Replace six panel door, fix new ironmongery, decorate	**495**	to	**845**

Single
Items
£

DOOR IS STICKING AND DOES NOT OPEN/CLOSE EASILY

SOLUTION
Ease sticking doors

Ease door without removal	**68**
Take down door, ease, adjust and rehang	**82**
Take down door, shave from bottom edge and rehang	**82**
Remove door, shave sides and top and bottom edges to fit opening, rehang	**115**
Ease and adjust door and frame of any size, adjust door stops, refix architrave and frame, overhaul ironmongery and leave in good working order	**98**

DOOR IS DAMAGED

SOLUTION
Repair door

Take down panelled door of any size, remove ironmongery and cover both sides with hardboard, refix ironmongery, adjust stops, rehang and decorate	**160**

DOOR FRAME IS DAMAGED OR LOOSE

SOLUTION

Take off door, remove ironmongery as necessary, replace door frame, decorate, refix door and ironmongery and leave in good working order	**285**
Take off door, remove ironmongery as necessary, replug and refix frame or lining, decorate, refix door and ironmongery and leave in good working order	**180**

	RANGE Type of Glass	
	£	£

GLAZING TO DOOR IS BROKEN

SOLUTION
Hack out broken glass and putty and reglaze single door

One pane size 150 x 150mm in half glazed panel door	**68**	to	**69**
All panes size 150 x 150mm in half glazed panel door	**95**	to	**130**
Half glazed panel door	**100**	to	**125**
Fully glazed panel door	**160**	to	**210**

	Single Items £

**PUTTY OR GLAZING BEADS ARE MISSING
OR LOOSE**

SOLUTION
Replace putty

One pane size 150 x 150mm in half glazed panel door	**63**
All panes size 150 x 150mm in half glazed panel door	**96**
Half glazed panel door	**66**
Fully glazed panel door	**69**

Replace glazing beads including decoration	
One pane size 150 x 150mm in half glazed panel door	**74**
All panes size 150 x 150mm in half glazed panel door	**235**
Half glazed panel door	**85**
Fully glazed panel door	**105**

	Single Items £

STAIRCASE TREADS, RISER, BALUSTERS ARE BADLY DAMAGED

SOLUTION
Replace

Straight flight softwood staircase	**1300**
Softwood handrail to stair flight	**215**
Softwood turned newel post	**155**
Hardwood turned newel post	**185**

HANDRAIL IS LOOSE

SOLUTION
Refix

Take off and refix handrail between newel posts	**75**

STAIRCASE TREADS, RISER, BALUSTERS ARE DAMAGED

SOLUTION
Repair

	Number of Units			
	1 £	2 £	3 £	5 £
Replace tread or riser to staircase	**98**	**135**	**175**	**255**
Replace plain baluster	**92**	**125**	**155**	**215**
Replace ornate baluster	**98**	**135**	**170**	**240**
Replug and screw handrail brackets	**71**	**79**	**88**	**105**

	Length of Worktop (m)			
	1	2	3	5
	£	£	£	£

WORKTOP IS BADLY SCORED/CHIPPED

SOLUTION
Replace worktop

	1	2	3	5
500mm wide	140	220	300	460
600mm wide	155	245	335	515

LAMINATE EDGING IS LOOSE OR MISSING

SOLUTION

	1	2	3	5
Replace plastic laminate edging 25mm wide	70	80	90	110

	Number of Units			
	1	2	3	5
	£	£	£	£

DOORS OR DRAWERS ARE DAMAGED

SOLUTION
Replace

	1	2	3	5
Replace damaged door using existing ironmongery	315	470	730	1170
Replace damaged drawer to floor unit to match existing	270	390	555	885

DOORS OR DRAWERS ARE BADLY FITTING

SOLUTION
Repair

	1	2	3	5
Take off, ease adjust and rehang door	76	89	100	125
Repair drawer, refix front and runners	82	105	125	165
Refix drawer, ease and adjust including runners	68	76	83	98

	Length (m)		
	1	2	3
GUTTERS ARE MISSING OR DAMAGED	£	£	£

SOLUTION
Replace gutters

	1	2	3
PVCu	135	170	205
Aluminium	150	200	250
Cast iron, including decoration	185	270	355

**RAINWATER DOWN PIPES ARE MISSING
OR DAMAGED**

SOLUTION
Replace pipes

	1	2	3
PVCu	125	155	185
Aluminium	155	210	265
Cast iron, including decoration	195	295	395

**RAINWATER FITTINGS ARE MISSING
OR DAMAGED**

SOLUTION
Replace head/hopper

	1	2	3
Cast aluminium, powder coated finish	125	185	245
Fabricated aluminium, powder coated finish	185	305	425
Cast iron, including decoration	110	160	210

Replace shoes

	1	2	3
PVCu	90	115	140
Aluminium	105	150	195
Cast iron	110	155	200

Replace balloon grating

	1	2	3
PVCu	68	77	86

Replace gutter brackets

	1	2	3
PVCu	68	77	86
Galvanised repair bracket	77	92	110

GUTTER JOINTS ARE LEAKING	Fittings (number)		
	1	2	3
	£	£	£

SOLUTION

	1	2	3
Apply mastic sealant to gutter joint	**74**	**87**	**100**

RANGE	RANGE		
	House Type		
	Terraced	Semi-Detached	Detached
GUTTERS ARE OVERFLOWING	£	£	£

SOLUTION
Clean out gutters, outlets etc

	Terraced	Semi-Detached	Detached
ONE ELEVATION	**130**	**140**	**190**
WHOLE HOUSE	**195**	**290**	**565**

Realign gutters
PVCu

	Terraced	Semi-Detached	Detached
ONE ELEVATION	**240**	**300**	**495**
WHOLE HOUSE	**415**	**715**	**1540**

Metal

	Terraced	Semi-Detached	Detached
ONE ELEVATION	**290**	**360**	**605**
WHOLE HOUSE	**515**	**885**	**1910**

Realign down pipes
PVCu

	Terraced	Semi-Detached	Detached
ONE ELEVATION	**235**	**235**	**260**
TWO ELEVATIONS	**285**	**285**	**315**

Metal

	Terraced	Semi-Detached	Detached
ONE ELEVATION	**285**	**285**	**315**
TWO ELEVATIONS	**500**	**500**	**565**

**NO SOAKAWAY TO RAINWATER DOWNPIPE
OR EXISTING SOAKAWAY OF INSUFFICIENT SIZE**

SOLUTION

	Single Items £
Enlarge or form new soakaway Excavate pit approx 1000 x 1000 x 1200mm, fill with selected hardcore and top with concrete bed on polythene sheeting and sand blinding	**300**

	Length (m)		
	1	2	5
	£	£	£

SOIL DOWN PIPES ARE MISSING OR DAMAGED

SOLUTION

	1	2	5
Replace pipes with PVCu pipework	**98**	**135**	**245**

	Single Items £

TRAPS TO SOIL PIPES ARE DAMAGED/BROKEN

SOLUTION
Replace

	Single Items £
32mm bottle trap and joints	**85**
40mm bottle trap and joints	**105**

BLOCKAGES OR OBSTRUCTIONS IN SANITARY FITTINGS

SOLUTION
Unblock

	Single Items £
Clear obstruction or blockage from WC pan, bath, shower, basin or sink, clean wastes and traps including removal and reassembling as necessary	**125**

	Single Items £

SEPTIC TANK IS LEAKING

SOLUTION
Replace

Excavate by hand, pit around existing tank, remove and install new septic tank, fixing lockable manhole cover and frame and connect to pipework

3750 litre capacity 2000mm diameter standard grade, 1000 mm depth to invert	**2980**
3750 litre capacity 2000mm diameter heavy duty grade, 1500 mm depth to invert	**4080**

DRAINS MAY BE BLOCKED

SOLUTION
Inspect drains

CCTV survey of drains including video and report, any reasonable run of domestic pipework	**180**

DRAINS ARE BLOCKED

SOLUTION

Clear obstructions in drain runs by water jetting, any reasonable run of domestic pipework	**150**

Rod drain from manhole, clean out and flush through, including replacing and resealing manhole cover

Drain run not exceeding 30m	**120**
Drain run over 30m	**135**

	Length of Pipe (m)			
	1	2	3	5
	£	£	£	£

DRAIN PIPES ARE BROKEN/CRACKED

SOLUTION
Replace broken length of vitrified or plastic pipe

100mm pipe

	1	2	3	5
Excavate through soft surface, average excavation depth 500mm deep, replace pipe, make good ground	150	230	310	405
Excavate through concrete or paving or tarmac surface, average excavation depth 500mm deep,replace pipe, make good surface to match existing	210	355	510	655
Excavate through soft surface, average excavation depth 1000mm deep, replace pipe, make good ground	180	295	410	580
Excavate through concrete or paving or tarmac surface, average excavation depth 1000mm deep, replace pipe, make good surface to match existing	240	415	470	825
Line damaged drain runs by inversion moulding, with grp lining	71	81	90	110

150mm pipe

	1	2	3	5
Excavate through soft surface, average excavation depth 500mm deep, replace pipe, make good ground	180	300	425	605
Excavate through concrete or paving or tarmac surface, average excavation depth 500mm deep, replace pipe, make good surface to match existing	240	425	645	1010
Excavate through soft surface, average excavation depth 1000mm deep, replace pipe, make good ground	215	360	520	815
Excavate through concrete or paving or tarmac surface, average excavation depth 1000mm deep, replace pipe, make good surface to match existing	275	410	690	960
Line damaged drain runs by inversion moulding with grp lining	89	120	150	205

	Single Items £

MANHOLE COVER AND FRAME ARE LOOSE

SOLUTION
Take off manhole cover not exceeding 600 x 600mm,
lift up frame and rebed on top of manhole in cement
mortar (1:3), reseal cover **105**

MANHOLE COVER AND FRAME ARE DAMAGED

SOLUTION
Renew damaged manhole cover and frame

Light duty cover and frame, clear opening 600 x 600mm **240**
Medium duty cover and frame, clear opening 600 x 450mm **240**
Medium duty cover and frame, clear opening 600 x 600mm **260**

BENCHING AT BOTTOM OF MANHOLE IS LOOSE/MISSING

SOLUTION
Break out defective benching to bottom of manhole and renew
in cement mortar trowelled smooth

460 x 690mm internally **155**
690 x 1140mm internally **185**

MANHOLE HAS COLLAPSED OR IS IN PROCESS OF COLLAPSING

SOLUTION
Take up existing cover and frame, demolish manhole and rebuild
concrete base, engineering brick sides in cement mortar,
concrete benching 100mm diameter vitrified clay channel bends,
not exceeding 2nr, 600 x 450mm manhole cover and frame

600 x 450 x 750mm deep internally **760**
600 x 450 x 1000mm deep internally **950**

	Single Items £

GULLY IS BLOCKED

SOLUTION
Clean out blockage **76**

GULLY GRID IS MISSING OR DAMAGED

SOLUTION
Replace cast iron gully grid **69**

GULLY KERB IS DAMAGED

SOLUTION
Replace broken precast concrete gully kerb **115**

GULLY IS DAMAGED

SOLUTION
Break out existing gully and install new back inlet gully with grating,
connect to existing 100mm drain, surround with concrete **405**

FRESH AIR INLET IS BROKEN OR MISSING

SOLUTION
Renew broken or missing aluminium fresh air inlet including mud flap **145**

DRIVEWAY IS BROKEN UP	Length of Drive/Footpath (m)			
	5	10	15	20
	£	£	£	£

SOLUTION
Replace driveway

Replace single width driveway

	5	10	15	20
75mm two coat rolled bitumen macadam	**720**	**1440**	**2160**	**2880**
Precast concrete slabs, 600 x 600	**865**	**1730**	**2600**	**3460**
Precast concrete coloured blocks, 200 x 100	**1510**	**3020**	**4530**	**6040**
Clay brick paviours 75mm thick (PC £40/100)	**1580**	**3160**	**4740**	**6320**
Clay brick paviours 25mm thick (PC £30/100)	**1460**	**2920**	**4380**	**5840**
Crazy paving broken precast concrete paving slabs	**1510**	**3020**	**4530**	**6040**
100mm thick insitu concrete with formwork to edges, to falls, tamped finish and trowelled edge	**1060**	**2120**	**3180**	**4240**

Replace double width driveway

	5	10	15	20
75mm two coat rolled bitumen macadam	**1440**	**2880**	**4320**	**5760**
Precast concrete slabs, 600 x 600	**1730**	**3460**	**5190**	**6920**
Precast concrete coloured blocks, 200 x 100	**3000**	**6000**	**9000**	**12000**
Clay brick paviours 75mm thick (PC £40/100)	**3160**	**6320**	**9480**	**12640**
Clay brick paviours 25mm thick (PC £30/100)	**2910**	**5820**	**8730**	**11640**
Crazy paving broken precast concrete paving slabs	**3030**	**6060**	**9090**	**12120**
100mm thick insitu concrete with formwork to edges, to falls, tamped finish and trowelled edge	**2110**	**4220**	**6330**	**8440**

FOOTPATH IS BROKEN UP

SOLUTION
Replace footpath

Replace footpath 1.2m wide

	5	10	15	20
75mm two coat rolled bitumen macadam	**350**	**700**	**1050**	**1400**
Precast concrete slabs, 600 x 600 x 50mm	**430**	**860**	**1290**	**1720**
Precast concrete coloured blocks, 200 x 100	**610**	**1220**	**1830**	**2440**
Clay brick paviours 75mm thick (PC £40/100)	**635**	**1270**	**1910**	**2540**
Clay brick paviours 25mm thick (PC £30/100)	**585**	**1170**	**1760**	**2340**
Crazy paving broken precast concrete paving slabs	**605**	**1210**	**1820**	**2420**
75mm thick insitu concrete with formwork to edges, to falls, tamped finish and trowelled edge	**405**	**810**	**1220**	**1620**

SURFACE OF DRIVEWAY IS BROKEN UP	Length of Drive/Footpath (m)			
	5 £	10 £	15 £	20 £

SOLUTION
Replace surfacing to driveway

Replace surfacing to single width driveway

	5	10	15	20
75mm two coat rolled bitumen macadam	530	1060	1590	2120
Precast concrete slabs, 600 x 600 x 50mm	670	1340	2010	2680
Precast concrete coloured blocks, 200 x 100	1320	2640	3960	5280
Clay brick paviours 75mm thick (PC £40/100)	1380	2760	4140	5520
Clay brick paviours 25mm thick (PC £30/100)	1270	2540	3810	5080
Crazy paving broken precast concrete paving slabs	1330	2660	3990	5320
100mm thick insitu concrete with formwork to edges, to falls, tamped finish, trowelled edge	865	1730	2600	3460
Take up and relay precast concrete slabs on dabs	570	1140	1710	2280

Replace surfacing to double width driveway

	5	10	15	20
75mm two coat rolled bitumen macadam	1060	2120	3180	4240
Precast concrete slabs, 600 x 600 x 50mm	1340	2680	4020	5360
Precast concrete coloured blocks, 200 x 100	2620	5240	7860	10480
Clay brick paviours 75mm thick (PC £40/100)	2780	5560	8340	11120
Clay brick paviours 25mm thick (PC £30/100)	2530	5060	7590	10120
Crazy paving broken precast concrete paving slabs	2640	5280	7920	10560
100mm thick insitu concrete with formwork to edges, to falls, tamped finish and trowelled edge	1730	3460	5190	6920

FOOTPATH IS BROKEN UP

SOLUTION
Replace surfacing to footpath

Replace surfacing to footpath 1.2m wide

	5	10	15	20
75mm two coat rolled bitumen macadam	270	420	635	845
Precast concrete slabs, 600 x 600 x 50mm	340	535	800	1070
Precast concrete coloured blocks, 200 x 100	525	1050	1580	2100
Clay brick paviours 75mm thick (PC £40/100)	555	1110	1670	2220
Clay brick paviours 25mm thick (PC £30/100)	510	1020	1530	2040
Crazy paving broken precast concrete paving slabs	530	1060	1590	2120
75mm thick insitu concrete with formwork to edges, to falls, tamped finish, trowelled edge	400	685	970	1255

DRIVEWAY OR FOOTPATH IS CRACKED

SOLUTION
Repair cracks

	Length of Crack (m)			
	1	2	3	5
	£	£	£	£
Fill crack in macadam or asphalt paving with hot bitumen	**175**	**185**	**195**	**215**
Rake out joint in brick paviors and repoint	**185**	**200**	**215**	**250**

DRIVEWAY OR FOOTPATH HAS POTHOLES

SOLUTION
Repair potholes

	Patches (number)			
	1	2	3	5
	£	£	£	£
Fill pothole in macadam or asphalt paving including preparing, making up levels and surfacing with mastic asphalt and limestone aggregate				
Small holes up to 0.1m²	**110**	**120**	**130**	**150**
Large holes up to 1m²	**150**	**230**	**310**	**470**

	Patches (number)			
	1	2	3	5
	£	£	£	£

DRIVEWAY OR FOOTPATH IS DAMAGED

SOLUTION
Repair damage to driveway or footpath

Take up and renew precast concrete paving slabs

	1	2	3	5
Patches, individual slabs	100	125	150	200
Patches, three slabs	145	210	275	405
Patches, five slabs	165	250	335	505

Take up and renew reconstructed stone paving slabs

	1	2	3	5
Patches, individual slabs	100	125	150	200
Patches, three slabs	150	220	290	470
Patches, five slabs	230	385	545	700

Take up and renew coloured concrete block

	1	2	3	5
patches, individual blocks	115	150	185	255
Patches, five blocks	265	470	565	940
Patches not exceeding 0.2m^2	105	135	155	225
Patches 0.2 to 0.5m^2	145	210	270	400
Patches 0.5 to 1m^2	210	340	485	775

Take up and renew brick paving

	1	2	3	5
Patches not exceeding 0.2m^2	98	130	150	200
Patches 0.2 to 0.5m^2	135	185	240	340
Patches 0.5 to 1m^2	175	265	375	535

TREES OR SHRUBS ARE TOO CLOSE TO BUILDING AND ARE CAUSING DAMP OR CRACKING TO WALLS

SOLUTION
Remove trees or shrubs

	Single Items £
Cut down and remove small trees and shrubs	**435**
Cut down and remove large trees	**1050**
Excavate around and remove tree stumps	
Small trees	**185**
Large trees	**280**

BRANCHES ARE OVERHANGING BUILDING, DRIVEWAY OR FOOTPATHS

SOLUTION
Cut back trees and shrubs

	Branches (number)			
	1 £	2 £	3 £	5 £
Pruning small branches not exceeding 1m long	**60**	**61**	**67**	**93**
Pruning large branches exceeding 1m long	**61**	**64**	**76**	**135**

BOUNDARY WALL IS FALLING DOWN

SOLUTION
Re-build freestanding brick wall

	Length of Wall (m)			
	1 £	2 £	3 £	5 £
Half brick thick wall				
1m high	185	310	435	635
1.5m high	255	445	715	1100
2m high	310	515	765	1250
One brick thick wall				
1m high	300	490	730	1220
1.5m high	425	730	1100	1830
2m high	490	980	1470	2440

RENDERING TO BOUNDARY WALL IS CRACKED OR LOOSE

SOLUTION
Repair rendering

	Length of Wall (m)			
	1 £	5 £	10 £	20 £
Hack off cracked and loose rendering and cart away, rake out joints and apply render				
1m high	145	415	840	1690
1.5m high	185	635	1265	2530
2m high	230	840	1680	3360

	Length of Fence (m)			
	1	5	10	20
	£	£	£	£

FENCING IS FALLING DOWN

SOLUTION
Replace fencing

Replace galvanised chain link fencing, with reinforced concrete posts

900mm high	170	560	1120	2240
1200mm high	180	610	1220	2440

Replace galvanised chain link fencing to existing posts

900mm high	80	175	290	460
1200mm high	83	185	310	510

Replace chestnut pale fencing, softwood posts

1000mm high with 2 or 3 wires	165	515	1030	2050

Replace close boarded fencing

Softwood posts	170	540	1080	2160
Oak posts	180	605	1210	2420
Reinforced concrete posts	195	685	1370	2740

Replace interwoven panel fencing

Softwood posts	170	540	1080	2160
Oak posts	185	640	1280	2560
Reinforced concrete posts	205	725	1450	2900

Replace gravel boards

Replace gravel boards with treated boards	71	135	190	300

	Panels or Posts (number)			
	1 £	2 £	3 £	5 £

FENCE PANELS ARE DAMAGED

SOLUTION
Replace interwoven or timber lap fencing

2m long panel and capping

	1	2	3	5
1m high	110	160	205	295
2m high	130	195	265	405

FENCE POSTS ARE BROKEN OR DAMAGED

SOLUTION
Replace intermediate post

2m long overall post

	1	2	3	5
Softwood	79	100	125	170
Oak	84	110	140	190
Concrete	95	135	175	255

GATES ARE MISSING, BROKEN OR DAMAGED

SOLUTION
Replace gates and posts

	Single Items £
Ledged and braced matchboard gate, including ironmongery	470
Framed, ledged and braced matchboard gate, including ironmongery	560
Single gate and posts, decorated, including stops and ironmongery	255
Double gates and posts, decorated, including ironmongery and stops, centre stop set in concrete	435

PART OF ROOF TIMBER IS DAMAGED
OR SPLIT

SOLUTION
Install softwood treated timber splints 1m long nailed to
both sides of existing damaged member

	Repairs (number)			
	1	2	4	6
	£	£	£	£
Rafters or purlins	**99**	**140**	**215**	**290**
Ridges	**110**	**155**	**250**	**345**

PART OF ROOF TIMBER IS DECAYED
OR SPLIT

SOLUTION
Cut out existing decayed, split etc. timber and
splice in softwood treated timber

	Length of Timber (m)		
	1	2	3
	£	£	£
Rafters or purlins	**160**	**250**	**340**
Ridges	**165**	**270**	**375**

COMPLETE ROOF TIMBER IS DECAYED
OR SPLIT

SOLUTION
Replace existing decayed, split etc. timber and
splice in softwood treated timber

		Length of Each Member (m)		
		4	5	6
		£	£	£
Rafters	single member	**345**	**430**	**515**
	two members	**690**	**860**	**1030**
Purlins	single member	**380**	**480**	**580**
	two members	**765**	**955**	**1145**

		Length of Each Member (m)		
		5	6	9
		£	£	£
Ridges		**525**	**630**	**945**

PART OF ROOF IS SAGGING

SOLUTION
Strengthen roof

Install additional softwood treated timber purlins

		Length of Each Member (m)		
		4	5	6
		£	£	£
Purlins	single member	**190**	**220**	**250**
	two members	**305**	**360**	**415**

Install additional softwood treated timber struts or ties

		Length of Each Member (m)		
		2	3	4
		£	£	£
	single strut	**135**	**160**	**185**
	two struts	**195**	**250**	**305**

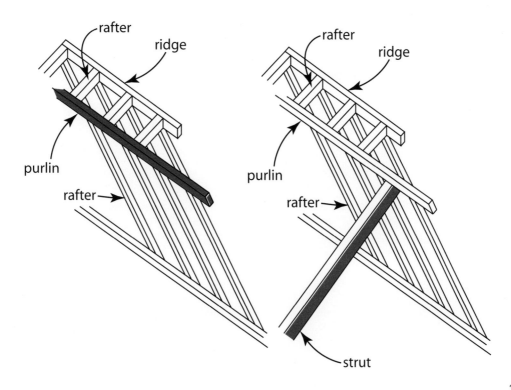

TILES/SLATES MISSING OR BROKEN ON ROOF

SOLUTION
Replace missing/broken tiles/slates

	Tiles/slates in One Location (m²)			
	1	2	5	6
	£	£	£	£
Plain clay tile	330	430	460	565
Concrete interlocking tile	280	330	470	520
Natural slate	395	555	770	930

TILES/SLATES MISSING OR BROKEN ON ROOF

SOLUTION
Replace missing/broken tiles/slates

	Tiles/slates in One Location (number)			
	1	2	5	6
	£	£	£	£
Plain clay tile	260	280	300	310
Concrete interlocking tile	260	280	300	310
Natural slate	265	290	315	325

TILES/SLATES LOOSE ON ROOF

SOLUTION

	1	2	5	6
Resecure tiles/slates	255	265	280	285

	Single Garage		Double Garage	
	Small	Large	Small	Large
	£	£	£	£

FELT TO FLAT ROOF IS LEAKING
Inspection recommends replacement

SOLUTION

Replace three layer felt roof	745	1220	1430	2310

**FELT TO FLAT ROOF IS LEAKING AND
BOARDING IS DAMAGED**
Inspection recommends replacement

SOLUTION

Replace three layer felt roof and boarding	1570	2570	3050	5030

**FELT TO FLAT ROOF IS LEAKING,
BOARDING AND INSULATION IS
DAMAGED**
Inspection recommends replacement

SOLUTION

Replace three layer felt roof, boarding and insulation	3200	5300	6330	10480

ASPHALT TO FLAT ROOF IS LEAKING
Inspection recommends replacement

SOLUTION

Hack up asphalt roofing and apply 19mm two coat work on felt and underlay	1250	2050	2420	3970

FELT TO FLAT ROOF IS LEAKING
Inspection recommends replacement

SOLUTION
Prepare existing mastic asphalt and overlay with

High performance felt	745	1210	1430	2310
Apply one coat bituminous paint	355	555	640	1010
Apply two coats bituminous paint	745	1210	1430	2310

	Repairs (number)		
	1	2	5
	£	£	£

SMALL PATCHES IN TOP LAYER OF FELT ROOF ARE DAMAGED

SOLUTION
Cut out defective layer, rebond to adjacent layers and cover with single layer felt

	1	2	5
Small patches not exceeding 0.5m^2	250	280	370
0.5 - 2m^2	265	310	445
2 - 5m^2	315	410	695

SMALL DEPRESSIONS HAVE APPEARED IN ROOF DECK

SOLUTION
Repair felt and boarding

	1	2	5
	285	340	530

AREAS OF FELT ROOF DEVOID OF CHIPPINGS

SOLUTION
Clear stone chippings, dress surface with compound and recover with chippings

	1	2	5
Small patches not exceeding 0.5m^2	250	280	355
0.5 - 2m^2	255	280	375
2 - 5m^2	280	340	525

BLISTERS OR CRACKS IN ASPHALT

SOLUTION

	1	2	5
Cut out detached blister and make good, 0.5m^2 area	250	275	345
Cut out crack and make good, per m run	255	285	375

ROOF IS LEAKING AT JUNCTION OF HOUSE AND GARAGE

Inspection recommends replacement of lead flashing

SOLUTION

	Length (m)			
	3 £	5 £	6 £	10 £
Replace flashing up to 225mm girth	**340**	**495**	**570**	**865**

ROOF IS LEAKING

Inspection recommends repair of lead flashing

SOLUTION

	Length (m)			
	1 £	2 £	3 £	5 £
Repair crack in sheeting, clean out and fill with solder	**160**	**185**	**210**	**260**
Refix existing lead flashings with new wedges and repoint with mortar	**175**	**215**	**255**	**340**

	Repairs (number)			
	1 £	2 £	3 £	5 £
Repair crack not exceeding 150mm long and fill with solder	**130**	**140**	**150**	**170**
Repair crack not exceeding 150 - 300mm long and fill with solder	**140**	**155**	**170**	**195**

EAVES OR VERGE BOARDING IS LOOSE

SOLUTION
Refix

	Single Garage		Double Garage	
	Small	Large	Small	Large
	£	£	£	£
Resecure eaves fascia, including decoration	**260**	**405**	**355**	**510**
Resecure eaves soffit, including decoration	**275**	**430**	**380**	**550**
Resecure eaves fascia and soffit, including decoration	**430**	**630**	**530**	**845**

	Single Garage		Double Garage	
	One Side	Both Sides	One Side	Both Sides
	£	£	£	£
Resecure verge boarding, including decoration	**165**	**215**	**215**	**310**

	RANGE	
	(Quality of Bricks)	
	£	£

BRICK FACES ARE DAMAGED OR CRACKED

SOLUTION
Replace defective bricks

Area of Patch (m²)			
1	**215**	to	**320**
2	**320**	to	**520**
3	**470**	to	**785**
5	**775**	to	**1310**

BRICKWORK HAS CRACK

SOLUTION

Cut out brickwork and replace with new brickwork

Length of Crack (m)			
1	**135**	to	**190**
2	**210**	to	**325**
3	**290**	to	**450**
5	**445**	to	**650**

INDIVIDUAL BRICKS ARE DAMAGED OR CRACKED

SOLUTION

Replace defective bricks

Bricks (number)			
1	**64**	to	**75**
2	**75**	to	**80**
5	**98**	to	**115**
10	**140**	to	**175**

HOLES IN BRICKWORK AFTER PIPES HAVE BEEN REMOVED

SOLUTION

	Holes (number)			
	1	2	3	5
	£	£	£	£
Fill holes				
Half brick thick walls	**90**	**100**	**110**	**130**

POINTING TO BRICK WALLS
IN POOR CONDITION

SOLUTION
Repoint

		Single Garage		Double Garage	
		Small £	Large £	Small £	Large £
Rake out joints and repoint					
	Front	325	325	630	630
	Rear	490	490	885	885
	Side	985	1640	985	1640
	All Walls	2790	4100	3490	4800

POINTING TO SMALL AREAS OF
BRICK WALLS IN POOR CONDITION

SOLUTION
Repoint

	Area of Patch (m²)			
	1 £	2 £	3 £	5 £
Pointing				
Rake out joints and repoint by machine	130	175	220	310
Rake out joints and repoint by hand	135	190	245	355

	Small Patch n.e. 0.5m² (number) £	Area (m²)		
		1 £	2 £	5 £

RENDERING IS DAMAGED

SOLUTION
Repair render

Hack out damaged render and rerender including decoration to match existing	150	195	265	475

PEBBLE DASH IS DAMAGED

SOLUTION
Repair pebble dash finish	150	180	245	435

BRICKWORK IS STAINED

SOLUTION
Sandblasting	98	140	260	460
Spraying with water	85	115	200	340

VERTICAL SHIPLAP CLADDING IS DAMAGED

SOLUTION
Replace damaged cladding

	Individual Board (number) £	Area (m²)		
		2 £	3 £	5 £
Replace softwood boarding	120	320	430	650
Replace pvc cladding	100	245	330	500

VERTICAL TILING IS MISSING OR DAMAGED

SOLUTION

	Area (m²)			
	2 £	3 £	5 £	6 £
Replace vertical tiles	310	425	650	765
Replace vertical slates	475	720	1210	1460

	Tiles in One Location (number)		
	1 £	5 £	10 £
Replace vertical tiles	125	180	245
Replace vertical slates	130	200	285

	Length of Crack (m)			
	1	2	3	5
	£	£	£	£

CONCRETE FLOOR IS CRACKED

SOLUTION
Clean out dust and debris and fill crack
with mortar

	1	2	3	5
Clean out dust and debris and fill crack with mortar	**63**	**70**	**76**	**89**

Cut out crack to form groove and fill
with mortar

	1	2	3	5
25 x 25mm groove	**70**	**83**	**95**	**120**
40 x 40mm groove	**76**	**93**	**115**	**150**

	RANGE	
	£	£

EXTERNAL DOOR IS DAMAGED

SOLUTION
Replace external door
Remove door, hang new door including refixing
ironmongery and decoration to both sides | **405** | to | **630** |
Remove door, hang new door including new
ironmongery and decoration to both sides | **580** | to | **950** |
Replace doors and frames
Replace timber door and frame with PVCu door
and frame | **930** | to | **1130** |

**EXTERNAL DOOR IRONMONGERY IS NOT
FUNCTIONING**

SOLUTION
Replace external door ironmongery
Renew rim lock and SAA lever furniture | **88** | to | **120** |
Renew steel butts, one and half pairs | **110** | to | **155** |
Renew mortice deadlock | **110** | to | **180** |
Renew cylinder mortice latch | **185** | to | **295** |
Renew letter plate | **115** | to | **130** |

GLASS TO DOOR IS BROKEN OR CRACKED

SOLUTION
Hack out broken glass and putty and reglaze single door
One pane size 150 x 150mm in half glazed panel door | **68** | to | **69** |
All panes size 150 x 150mm in half glazed panel door | **105** | to | **130** |
Half glazed panel door | **100** | to | **125** |
Fully glazed panel door | **160** | to | **210** |

GARAGE DOOR IS DAMAGED

Single
Items
£

SOLUTION
Dismantle up and over door, supply and fit new
aluminium door and decorate | **1630**
Take off doors and cart away, hang new framed,
ledged and braced softwood doors, clad one side
with v-jointed boarding and including furniture,
new frame and decorations | **1570**

	Single Items £

PUTTY OR GLAZING BEADS ARE MISSING OR LOOSE

SOLUTION
Replace putty
One pane size 150 x 150mm in half glazed panel door | **62**
All panes size 150 x 150mm in half glazed panel door | **95**
Half glazed panel door | **66**
Fully glazed panel door | **68**
Replace glazing beads including decoration
One pane size 150 x 150mm in half glazed panel door | **73**
All panes size 150 x 150mm in half glazed panel door | **235**
Half glazed panel door | **84**
Fully glazed panel door | **105**

DOORS AND FRAMES DAMAGED OR NOT CLOSING, THRESHOLDS UNSATISFACTORY

SOLUTION
Repair doors and frames
Ease door without removal | **69**
Take down door, ease, adjust and rehang | **82**
Take down door, shave 12mm from bottom edge and rehang | **82**
Remove door, shave sides and top and bottom edges to
fit opening, rehang | **115**
Ease and adjust doors and frames
Ease and adjust door and frame of any size, adjust door stops, refix
architrave and frame, overhaul ironmongery and leave in good
working order | **110**
Repair/replace door frames and thresholds
Take off door and rehang, remove and refix ironmongery as necessary,
make good decorations and leave in good working order
Repair single door and frame of any size | **160**
Replace softwood door frame | **320**
Replace hardwood threshold | **255**
Replace water bar
Galvanised steel bar bedded in mastic, to single door opening | **125**
Repoint one side with polysulphide sealant
Single door frame | **82**
Threshold | **66**
Insert external threshold seal with weather board strip
Single door opening | **110**
Single door opening to doors with water bar | **155**

	RANGE Approximate Window Size	
	600 x 900mm £	1200 x 1200mm £

WINDOW IS DAMAGED OR ROTTEN

SOLUTION
Replace window

Take out and install new double glazed window

PVCu casement window	**270**	to	**690**
PVCu sash window	**1040**	to	**1930**

Take out and install new single glazed window including decorating externally

Timber casement window	**390**	to	**550**
Timber sash window	**720**	to	**1130**
Metal casement window	**405**	to	**660**

Take out and install new double glazed window including decorating externally

Timber casement window	**545**	to	**770**
Timber sash window	**815**	to	**1300**
Metal casement window	**625**	to	**825**

	Single Items £

OPENING WINDOWS ARE STICKING

SOLUTION

Ease opening casement or sash without removal	**68**
Renew sash cord to single sash	**105**
Renew both sets of sash cords to single window	**115**

SECONDARY GLAZING UNIT DOES NOT OPERATE

SOLUTION

Remove and refit unit, of any size	**73**

OPENING WINDOWS AND IRONMONGERY STICKING, PUTTY AND BEADS ROTTEN OR MISSING

SOLUTION

Ease and adjust casement or sash window, overhaul ironmongery, renew beads with putty and sprigs, adjust stops and beads	**110**

WINDOW IN POOR CONDITION

SOLUTION

Piece in damaged area of frame, sill or casement with new timber, renew broken glass as necessary, overhaul or provide new ironmongery	**195**

WINDOW SILL IS ROTTEN

SOLUTION

Cut out sill complete and replace, including decoration

600mm long	**185**
1800mm long	**330**

POINTING AROUND WINDOW FRAME IS MISSING OR LOOSE

SOLUTION

Repoint frame, up to window size 1800 x 1800mm	**90**
Repoint window sills, 600 - 1800mm long	**68**

	Single Items £

IRONMONGERY TO WINDOW IS MISSING OR INOPERABLE

SOLUTION
Renew casement stay and fastener · **85**

	RANGE Approximate Pane Size		
	300 x 600mm £		900 x 900mm £

WINDOW PANE IS BROKEN

SOLUTION
Remove glass and putty, prepare and reglaze · **93** · to · **170**

PUTTY AROUND PANE IS MISSING OR LOOSE

SOLUTION
Replace putty · **69** · to · **75**

GLAZING BEADS AROUND PANE ARE MISSING OR DAMAGED

SOLUTION
Replace glazing beads including decoration · **96** · to · **130**

2:2 SERVICES

ELECTRICITY

	Fittings (number)			
	1 £	2 £	3 £	5 £

CIRCUIT TO APPLIANCE IS FAULTY
Inspection recommends rewiring

SOLUTION

	1	2	3	5
Rewire circuit, from heater to fuse box, maximum cable length 12m	185	330	475	765
Rewire circuit, from heater to power connection, maximum cable length 3m	93	150	200	300
Renew thermostat	115	185	255	400

	Length of Cable/Conduit (m)			
	1 £	2 £	3 £	5 £

CIRCUIT TO POWER POINT/LIGHT POINT IS FAULTY
Inspection recommends rewiring

SOLUTION

	1	2	3	5
Renew wiring to power or lighting, in conduit	54	67	79	105

	Fittings (number)			
	1 £	2 £	3 £	5 £

FITTINGS ARE FAULTY
Inspection recommends rewiring

SOLUTION

	1	2	3	5
Refix power point including checking and reconnecting wiring	58	74	90	120
Replace damaged surface mounted socket outlet	79	115	150	220
Replace damaged flush mounted socket outlet cover plate only	75	110	140	205
Replace damaged flush mounted socket outlet including box	90	135	180	265

	Single Items £

FITTINGS ARE FAULTY
Inspection recommends replacing/overhauling

SOLUTION
Power

Faulty consumer control unit	
Overhaul and check consumer control unit	**56**
Renew consumer control unit	**310**
Renew MCB in existing consumer unit	**63**
Replace damaged fittings	
Renew cooker control panel, flush fitting	**99**

Lighting

Overhaul faulty lighting main switch including isolating and reconnecting supply, cleaning contacts and testing	**79**
Trace fault on wiring circuit	**75**

Replace faulty equipment

Renew time control switch and test	**145**
Renew immersion heater, isolate supply, drain tank, disconnect and connect heater and test top heater	**99**
Bottom heater	**120**
Instant water heaters	
Inspect and repair faulty heater	**73**
Supply and fit new instant hand wash unit	**315**

EXTERNAL WATER MAIN INSIDE
PROPERTY BOUNDARY IS LEAKING

SOLUTION
Replace pipe

	Length of Pipework (m)			
	5	10	15	20
	£	£	£	£
Replace pipe, excavating and making good in the following surfaces				
Soft surface	345	685	1030	1370
Concrete or paving slabs surface	540	1080	1620	2160
Tarmac surface	590	1180	1770	2360
Clay paviors surface	650	1300	1950	2600

	Length of Pipework (m)			
	1	2	3	5
	£	£	£	£
Replace short length of pipe, excavating and making good in the following surfaces				
Soft surface	130	195	260	395
Concrete or paving slabs surface	175	275	380	525
Tarmac surface	180	295	410	570
Clay paviors surface	190	320	450	645

WATER SUPPLY PIPEWORK INSIDE
PROPERTY IS LEAKING
Inspection recommends total replacement

SOLUTION

	RANGE		
	£		£
Replace all hot and cold water pipework, storage cistern, expansion tank, hot water cylinder, immersion heater, connecting pipework to existing sanitary fittings	2370	to	3570
As above, but including new sanitary fittings	4700	to	9950

	Length of Pipework (m)			
	1	2	5	10
	£	£	£	£

WATER PIPES LEAKING

SOLUTION
Remove old pipe and fix new copper pipe
including all cutting and bending

Soft surface	**130**	**195**	**345**	**685**
Concrete or paving slabs surface	**175**	**285**	**540**	**1080**
Tarmac surface	**180**	**295**	**590**	**1180**
Clay paviors surface	**190**	**305**	**650**	**1300**

WATER PIPES BURST

SOLUTION

Cut out and replace exposed copper pipework	**130**	**190**	–	–
Cut out and replace concealed copper pipework, behind access panel or the like	**155**	**245**	–	–

	Single Items £

FITTINGS ARE FAULTY
Inspection recommends replacing/overhauling

SOLUTION

Replace cold water storage cistern or tank and lid, 27l capacity	**285**
Replace cold water storage cistern or tank and lid, 45l capacity	**490**
Remove existing and install hot water cylinder size 1200 x 450mm and connect all pipework	**430**
Remove existing and install immersion heater	**160**

FITTINGS ARE FAULTY, CARRY OUT REPAIR

SOLUTION

Replace ball cock to cold water tank	**140**
Replace 32mm bottle trap and joints	**81**
Replace 40mm bottle trap and joints	**105**
Renew one 2-piece clip to copper pipe	**67**
Renew two 2-piece clips to copper pipe	**73**
Renew three 2-piece clips to copper pipe	**79**

	Suites £

FITTINGS ARE FAULTY
Inspection recommends replacing complete suites

SOLUTION
Rates for appliances include for standard range components, coloured white

Bathroom

Basin and pressed steel bath	1380
Basin and plastic bath	1540
Low level cistern WC with seat, basin and pressed steel bath	2100
Low level cistern WC with seat, basin and plastic bath	2260

Shower Room

Low level cistern WC with seat, basin and plastic shower tray	1720
Low level cistern WC with seat, basin and ceramic shower tray	1870

Cloakroom

Low level cistern WC with seat and basin	1240

Kitchen

Stainless steel sink with single bowl and drainer	575
Belfast sink	710

INDIVIDUAL FITTINGS ARE FAULTY
Inspection recommends replacing

SOLUTION
Rates for appliances include for standard range components,
coloured white

Replace fittings, complete with taps and waste and connecting all services

WC suite with low level cistern and seat	680
Wash basin	510
Belfast sink	710
Stainless steel sink with single bowl and drainer	575
Bath pressed steel	875
Bath plastic	1040
Shower tray plastic	495
Shower tray ceramic	650
Toilet seat and cover	130

	Single Items £

INDIVIDUAL FITTINGS ARE FAULTY
Inspection recommends repair

SOLUTION

Shower tray, remove mastic and reseal perimeter	**92**
Replace shower head and bracket	**90**
Replace flexible shower hose	**85**
Renew ball valve including plastic float	**140**
Renew plastic syphonage unit to high or low level cisterns	**125**
Fit replacement washer to ball valve	**78**
Renew joint of WC to soil pipe with 102mm pan connector	**200**
Take off WC seat and cover provide new fixing kit and refix	**115**
Remove existing seat to WC pan and replace with new seat and cover	**130**
Refix loose sanitary fitting, rescrew brackets to wall	**105**
Fit replacement washer to tap	**78**
Replace faulty basin pillar tap with new to match existing	**130**
Replace faulty bib tap with new to match existing	**135**

BLOCKAGE IN FITTINGS

SOLUTION

Clear obstruction or blockage from bath, shower, basin, or sink, clean wastes and traps including removal and reassembling as necessary	**110**
Clear obstruction or blockage from WC pan, including cleaning and any necessary removal and reassembling	**125**

	RANGE	
£		£

HEATING SYSTEM IS NOT WORKING
Inspection recommends replacement

SOLUTION
Replace heating system

Replace heating system excluding pipework
Wall mounted boiler, single and double panel radiators,
wall thermostat and programmer

Clockwork programmer	**4420**	to	**6980**
Digital programmer	**5150**	to	**7710**

Replace heating system including pipework
Wall mounted boiler, single and double panel radiators,
pipework, wall thermostat and programmer

Clockwork programmer	**6405**	to	**10510**
Digital programmer	**7140**	to	**11240**

	Single Items £

INDIVIDUAL FITTINGS ARE FAULTY
Inspection recommends replacing or repairing

SOLUTION
Replace fittings

Replace boilers

Replace wall mounted boiler, including draining down system and connecting to flue and pipework	**1720**
Replace free standing boiler, including draining down system and connecting to flue and pipework	**4770**

Replace radiators including reconnection and rebalancing

Single panel 400 x 600mm	**185**
Single panel 500 x 1000mm	**235**
Single panel 600 x 1800mm	**360**
Double panel 400 x 500mm	**250**
Double panel 500 x 1200mm	**405**
Double panel 600 x 1600mm	**535**

Replace radiator valves

Replace radiator valves	**110**
Replace thermostatic radiator valve	**125**

Replace central heating controls

Cylinder thermostat	**94**
Wall thermostat	**98**
Programmer (clockwork)	**230**
Programmer (digital)	**960**

Cleaning out central heating system

Powerflush system	**435**

Repair storage heaters

Overhaul storage heaters, including inspecting fusible link, replace thermostat, resetting thermal cutout and checking cable and testing	**155**

2:3 FINISHES

INTERIOR
Ceilings

	RANGE		
	House Type		
	Terraced	Semi-Detached	Detached
	£	£	£

CEILING IS BADLY DAMAGED OR COLLAPSED

SOLUTION
Replace ceiling

Apply plaster skim and decorate two coats
of emulsion paint

	Terraced	Semi-Detached	Detached
GROUND FLOOR	360	800	2540
FIRST FLOOR	440	885	2620
WHOLE HOUSE	800	1690	5160

Replace lath and plaster or plasterboard
ceiling with plasterboard and apply two
coats of emulsion paint

	Terraced	Semi-Detached	Detached
GROUND FLOOR	860	2040	6500
FIRST FLOOR	1060	2250	6720
WHOLE HOUSE	1920	4290	13220

CEILING IS DAMAGED OR UNEVEN

SOLUTION
Construct an independent ceiling

Plasterboard on softwood battens and
decorate two coats of emulsion paint

	Terraced	Semi-Detached	Detached
GROUND FLOOR	825	1850	5860
FIRST FLOOR	1030	2040	6060
WHOLE HOUSE	1860	3890	11920

	Ceilings to Room Room Size		
	3 x 3m £	4 x 4m £	8 x 4m £

CEILING IS BADLY DAMAGED OR COLLAPSED

SOLUTION
Replace ceiling

	3 x 3m	4 x 4m	8 x 4m
Replace plasterboard ceiling and emulsion paint	455	810	1620
Replace lath and plaster ceiling and emulsion paint	485	860	1720

CEILING HAS SMALL CRACKS AND HOLES IN WHOLE AREA OF ROOM

SOLUTION
Repair ceiling

	3 x 3m	4 x 4m	8 x 4m
Apply plaster skim and decorate two coats emulsion paint	280	430	675

CEILING HAS SMALL CRACKS AND HOLES

SOLUTION
Repair ceiling

	Patches (number)			
	not exceeding 0.5m^2		not exceeding 1m^2	
	1 £	2 £	1 £	2 £
Replace plasterboard ceiling and emulsion paint	125	180	135	185
Replace lath and plaster ceiling and emulsion paint	135	190	175	270

	Length of Crack (m)			
	1 £	2 £	3 £	5 £
Rake out and fill in crack in plaster ceiling not exceeding 75mm wide	105	115	125	140

	Room Size	RANGE Quality of Materials		
	m	£		£

FLOOR COVERING IS DAMAGED

SOLUTION
Replace floor covering

Carpet	3 x 3	655	to	845
	4 x 4	1160	to	1510
	8 x 4	2330	to	3010
Carpet and underlay	3 x 3	740	to	930
	4 x 4	1310	to	1650
	8 x 4	2620	to	3310
PVC flooring, sheeting or tiles	3 x 3	605	to	710
	4 x 4	1080	to	1260
	8 x 4	2160	to	2520
Quarry tiles	3 x 3	990		
	4 x 4	1760		
	8 x 4	3520		
Vitrified ceramic floor tiles	3 x 3	1370		
	4 x 4	2430		
	8 x 4	4870		
Wood flooring	3 x 3	680	to	990
	4 x 4	1210	to	1760
	8 x 4	2410	to	3520

	Patches not exceeding 0.5m² (number)			
	1	2	3	5
	£	£	£	£

**FLOOR COVERING IS DAMAGED IN
SMALL AREAS**

SOLUTION
Replace floor covering in damaged areas

PVC floor tiles	77	93	110	140
Quarry tiles	160	265	370	515
Vitrified ceramic floor tiles	210	360	510	745
Wood strip flooring	105	145	185	265
Wood block flooring	120	180	235	350

	Skirtings to Room (one door opening) Room Size		
	3 x 3m £	4 x 4m £	8 x 4m £

SKIRTING IS DAMAGED OR MISSING

SOLUTION
Replace skirting

19 x 100mm chamfered and rounded softwood skirting, decorated	340	460	705
25 x 175mm torus section softwood skirting, decorated	360	490	745
Clay quarry tile coved skirting 150mm high	610	840	1290

SKIRTING IS LOOSE

SOLUTION
Refix loose skirtings

Resecure loose skirtings	110	130	160
Resecure loose skirtings and redecorate	215	270	385

	Skirting in Short Lengths		
	1m long £	2m long £	3m long £

SHORT LENGTHS OF SKIRTING ARE DAMAGED OR MISSING

SOLUTION
Replace skirting

19 x 100mm chamfered and rounded softwood skirting, decorated	95	125	155
25 x 175mm torus section softwood skirting, decorated	100	130	160
Clay quarry tile coved skirting 150mm high	120	175	230

SHORT LENGTHS OF SKIRTING ARE LOOSE

SOLUTION
Refix loose skirtings

Resecure loose skirtings	67	71	75
Resecure loose skirtings, repaint	74	89	105

	RANGE		
	Quality of Materials		
	£		£

WALL PLASTER IS LOOSE, CRACKED OR MISSING

SOLUTION

	Room Size (m)			
Rerender or replaster walls	3 x 3	**1350**	to	**2610**
	4 x 4	**1850**	to	**3570**
	8 x 4	**2690**	to	**5230**
Rerender or replaster walls including new skirting and decoration	3 x 3	**1930**	to	**3180**
	4 x 4	**2630**	to	**4370**
	8 x 4	**4180**	to	**6990**

	Walls			
Rerender or replaster walls	2.75m high			
	3m long	**365**	to	**705**
	4m long	**500**	to	**970**
	5m long	**640**	to	**1240**
	8m long	**1050**	to	**2050**
Rerender or replaster walls including new skirting and decoration	3m long	**525**	to	**865**
	4m long	**715**	to	**1180**
	5m long	**905**	to	**1500**
	8m long	**1480**	to	**2360**

PATCHES OF WALL PLASTER ARE LOOSE, CRACKED OR MISSING

SOLUTION

Replaster patches in wall plaster

	Number of Patches (number)			
Small patches not exceeding 0.5m2 in area	1	**105**	to	**120**
	2	**165**	to	**180**
	3	**210**	to	**240**
	5	**300**	to	**360**
Small patches not exceeding 1m2 in area	1	**135**	to	**175**
	2	**205**	to	**290**
	3	**275**	to	**405**
	5	**415**	to	**630**

CRACKS IN PLASTER

SOLUTION
Repair cracks

	Length of Crack (m)			
	1	2	3	5
	£	£	£	£
Rake out and refill crack in plaster	**67**	**75**	**83**	**98**

	Number of Cracks (number)			
	1	2	3	5
	£	£	£	£
Rake out and refill crack in plaster 1m long	**67**	**74**	**81**	**93**

	RANGE	
	Quality of Materials	
	£	£

WALL TILING IN POOR CONDITION, TILES MISSING

SOLUTION

Replace wall tiles	Tiles (m²)			
600mm high to splashbacks 1m long	0.6	**115**	to	**120**
600mm high to splashbacks 2m long	1.2	**170**	to	**180**
600mm high to splashbacks 3m long	1.8	**225**	to	**240**
600mm high to splashbacks 5m long	3	**335**	to	**360**
Walls 2.75m high, 2m long	5.5	**510**	to	**555**
Walls 2.75m high, 3m long	8	**735**	to	**810**
Walls 2.75m high, 4m long	11	**1010**	to	**1120**
Walls 2.75m high, 5m long	14	**1280**	to	**1420**
1.2m high to bathrooms	11	**1010**	to	**1120**
Full height to showers	10	**920**	to	**1020**
Full height to bathrooms	25	**2290**	to	**2540**

PATCHES OF WALL TILING IN POOR CONDITION, TILES MISSING

SOLUTION

Replace wall tiles in small areas

Number of
Patches

Patches not exceeding 0.5m² area

1	**145**	to	**150**
2	**190**	to	**200**
3	**230**	to	**240**
5	**335**	to	**365**

Patches not exceeding 1.0m² area

1	**185**	to	**200**
2	**310**	to	**335**
3	**435**	to	**470**
5	**625**	to	**685**

2:4 REDECORATIONS

EXTERIOR
Cladding

Height of Cladding (m)	Length of Cladding (m)		
	3 £	5 £	8 £

VERTICAL CLADDING IS IN POOR DECORATIVE ORDER

SOLUTION
Prepare and redecorate timber cladding at low level
Clean down, one undercoat, one finishing coat oil paint

1.2	120	160	220
3.0	260	355	435

Clean down, one coat polyurethane varnish

1.2	98	125	165
3.0	190	260	365

Clean down, one coat woodstain system

1.2	135	185	255
3.0	305	425	540

Rub down, prepare and paint one coat knotting and primer, two undercoats, one finishing coat oil paint

1.2	165	235	340
3.0	410	585	850

Burn off paint, prepare and paint one coat knotting and primer, two undercoats, one finishing coat oil paint

1.2	215	310	460
3.0	505	740	1090

Height of Cladding (m)	Length of Cladding (m)		
	3 £	5 £	8 £

VERTICAL CLADDING IS IN POOR DECORATIVE ORDER

SOLUTION
Prepare and redecorate timber cladding at high level
Clean down, one undercoat, one finishing coat oil paint

1.2	160	200	260
3.0	360	450	535
6.0	540	820	1240

Clean down, one coat polyurethane varnish

1.2	140	165	200
3.0	290	360	465
6.0	445	680	1030

Clean down, one coat woodstain system

1.2	180	225	295
3.0	400	515	635
6.0	600	920	1400

Rub down, prepare and paint one coat knotting and primer, two undercoats, one finishing coat oil paint

1.2	205	275	380
3.0	510	685	890
6.0	755	1160	1770

Burn off paint, prepare and paint one coat knotting and primer, two undercoats, one finishing coat oil paint

1.2	255	355	505
3.0	575	860	1290
6.0	975	1500	2290

	Doors	
	One Side £	Both Sides £

DOORS ARE IN POOR DECORATIVE ORDER

SOLUTION
Prepare and redecorate doors

	One Side £	Both Sides £
Clean down, one undercoat, one finishing coat oil paint		
flush or half glazed	90	125
fully glazed	85	105
Clean down, one coat polyurethane varnish		
flush or half glazed	80	100
fully glazed	75	90
Clean down, one coat woodstain system		
flush or half glazed	95	135
fully glazed	80	95
Rub down, prepare and paint one coat knotting and primer, two undercoats, one finishing coat oil paint		
flush or half glazed	125	190
fully glazed	90	120
Burn off paint, prepare and paint one coat knotting and primer, two undercoats, one finishing coat oil paint		
flush or half glazed	160	265
fully glazed	155	250

	Door Frames	
	One Side £	Both Sides £

DOOR FRAMES ARE IN POOR DECORATIVE ORDER

SOLUTION
Prepare and redecorate door frames

	One Side £	Both Sides £
Clean down, one undercoat, one finishing coat oil paint	110	165
Clean down, one coat polyurethane varnish	95	125
Clean down, one coat woodstain system	135	180
Rub down, prepare and paint one coat knotting and primer, two undercoats, one finishing coat oil paint	165	270
Burn off paint, prepare and paint one coat knotting and primer, two undercoats, one finishing coat oil paint	230	400

	Door and Frame			
	Without Fanlight		With Fanlight	
	One Side	Both Sides	One Side	Both Sides
	£	£	£	£

DOORS AND FRAMES ARE IN POOR DECORATIVE ORDER

SOLUTION
Prepare and redecorate doors

Clean down, one undercoat, one finishing coat oil paint

flush or half glazed doors	155	240	180	285
fully glazed doors	150	220	165	265

Clean down, one coat polyurethane varnish

flush or half glazed doors	120	170	135	190
fully glazed doors	115	165	130	190

Clean down, one coat woodstain system

flush or half glazed doors	160	260	185	300
fully glazed doors	140	220	165	265

Rub down, prepare and paint one coat knotting and primer, two undercoats, one finishing coat oil paint

flush or half glazed doors	250	415	290	500
fully glazed doors	215	345	255	430

Burn off paint, prepare and paint one coat knotting and primer, two undercoats, one finishing coat oil paint

flush or half glazed doors	365	635	435	770
fully glazed doors	355	615	415	750

	RANGE Approx Window Size (mm)		
	600 x 900 £		1500 x 1200 £

WINDOWS ARE IN POOR DECORATIVE ORDER

SOLUTION
Prepare and redecorate windows

Low level

	600 x 900 £		1500 x 1200 £
Clean down, one undercoat, one finishing coat oil paint	**74**	to	**125**
Clean down, one coat polyurethane varnish	**71**	to	**110**
Clean down, one coat woodstain system	**74**	to	**125**
Rub down, prepare and paint one coat knotting and primer, two undercoats, one finishing coat oil paint	**81**	to	**190**
Burn off paint, prepare and paint one coat knotting and primer, two undercoats, one finishing coat oil paint	**82**	to	**195**

High level

	600 x 900 £		1500 x 1200 £
Clean down, one undercoat, one finishing coat oil paint	**105**	to	**160**
Clean down, one coat polyurethane varnish	**99**	to	**135**
Clean down, one coat woodstain system	**105**	to	**150**
Rub down, prepare and paint one coat knotting and primer, two undercoats, one finishing coat oil paint	**140**	to	**240**
Burn off paint, prepare and paint one coat knotting and primer, two undercoats, one finishing coat oil paint	**150**	to	**250**

WINDOWS ARE IN POOR DECORATIVE ORDER	Per Elevation - Window Sizes			
	Example A £	Example B £	Example C £	Example D £

SOLUTION
Prepare and redecorate windows

Clean down, one undercoat, one finishing coat oil paint

	A	B	C	D
Windows with one pane	220	270	290	300
Windows with two or more panes	235	270	295	300
Georgian type windows with small panes	345	450	515	545

Clean down, one coat polyurethane varnish

	A	B	C	D
Windows with one pane	205	255	270	275
Windows with two or more panes	220	270	295	300
Georgian type windows with small panes	285	360	395	415

Clean down, one coat woodstain system

	A	B	C	D
Windows with one pane	205	255	270	275
Windows with two or more panes	235	295	325	335
Georgian type windows with small panes	320	410	465	495

Rub down, prepare and paint one coat knotting and primer, two undercoats, one finishing coat oil paint

	A	B	C	D
Windows with one pane	295	370	405	445
Windows with two or more panes	325	415	470	505
Georgian type windows with small panes	475	645	805	835

Burn off paint, prepare and paint one coat knotting and primer, two undercoats, one finishing coat oil paint

	A	B	C	D
Windows with one pane	305	390	425	470
Windows with two or more panes	345	450	510	540
Georgian type windows with small panes	550	775	920	975

Number and sizes of windows in tables above

Example A	two 1500 x 1200mm, one 1200 x 1200mm
Example B	four 1500 x 1200mm, one 900 x 900mm
Example C	one 1800 x 1800mm, two 1500 x 1200mm
	one 1200 x 1200mm, one 1200 x 900mm
Example D	one 1800 x 1800mm, four 1500 x 1200mm

	RANGE		
	House Type		
	Terraced	Semi-Detached	Detached
WINDOWS ARE IN POOR DECORATIVE ORDER	£	£	£

SOLUTION
Prepare and redecorate windows

Clean down, one undercoat, one finishing coat oil paint

	Terraced	Semi-Detached	Detached
Windows with one pane	265	395	1170
Windows with two or more panes	305	450	1340
Georgian type windows with small panes	525	800	2590

Clean down, one coat polyurethane varnish

	Terraced	Semi-Detached	Detached
Windows with one pane	240	355	1030
Windows with two or more panes	270	400	1180
Georgian type windows with small panes	380	570	1810

Clean down, one coat woodstain system

	Terraced	Semi-Detached	Detached
Windows with one pane	240	360	1030
Windows with two or more panes	300	445	1340
Georgian type windows with small panes	455	690	2220

Rub down, prepare and paint one coat knotting and
primer, two undercoats, one finishing coat oil paint

	Terraced	Semi-Detached	Detached
Windows with one pane	345	520	1590
Windows with two or more panes	420	645	2010
Georgian type windows with small panes	700	1080	3530

Burn off paint, prepare and paint one coat knotting
and primer, two undercoats, one finishing coat oil paint

	Terraced	Semi-Detached	Detached
Windows with one pane	385	575	1810
Windows with two or more panes	485	710	2250
Georgian type windows with small panes	870	1340	4470

| | RANGE | | |
| | House Type | | |
	Terraced	Semi-Detached	Detached
WINDOWS, DOORS AND FRAMES ARE IN POOR DECORATIVE ORDER	£	£	£

SOLUTION
Prepare and redecorate windows, doors and frames

Clean down, one undercoat, one finishing coat oil paint

	Terraced	Semi-Detached	Detached
Windows with one pane	450	580	1360
Windows with two or more panes	490	635	1530
Georgian type windows with small panes	710	990	2780

Clean down, one coat polyurethane varnish

	Terraced	Semi-Detached	Detached
Windows with one pane	355	475	1150
Windows with two or more panes	385	515	1300
Georgian type windows with small panes	495	690	1920

Clean down, one coat woodstain system

	Terraced	Semi-Detached	Detached
Windows with one pane	440	555	1230
Windows with two or more panes	500	645	1540
Georgian type windows with small panes	655	890	2420

Rub down, prepare and paint one coat knotting and primer, two undercoats, one finishing coat oil paint

	Terraced	Semi-Detached	Detached
Windows with one pane	720	890	1960
Windows with two or more panes	795	1020	2380
Georgian type windows with small panes	1080	1450	3910

Burn off paint, prepare and paint one coat knotting and primer, two undercoats, one finishing coat oil paint

	Terraced	Semi-Detached	Detached
Windows with one pane	995	1180	2420
Windows with two or more panes	1090	1320	2860
Georgian type windows with small panes	1480	1950	5080

CEILING IS BADLY STAINED/IN POOR DECORATIVE ORDER

SOLUTION
Redecorate ceiling

	RANGE House Type		
	Terraced	Semi-Detached	Detached
	£	£	£
Ceiling decoration to whole house			
Lining paper and emulsion paint	930	1960	6030
Embossed paper and emulsion paint	1050	2200	6760
Emulsion paint	285	615	1900
Ceiling decoration to ground floor			
Lining paper and emulsion paint	415	930	2960
Embossed paper and emulsion paint	470	1050	3330
Emulsion paint	190	355	930
Ceiling decoration to first floor			
Lining paper and emulsion paint	515	1030	3070
Embossed paper and emulsion pain.	580	1160	3430
Emulsion paint	225	380	960

	Ceilings to Room Room Size		
	3 x 3m	4 x 4m	8 x 4m
	£	£	£
Emulsion paint to existing painted ceilings	130	190	320
Emulsion paint to existing artex ceilings	190	295	535
Remove expanded polystyrene tiles, prepare and apply emulsion paint to ceiling	270	370	740
Replace paper			
Hang lining paper and emulsion paint	205	395	790
Hang embossed paper and emulsion paint	235	440	880

	Ceilings to Room Room Size		
	3 x 3m £	4 x 4m £	8 x 4m £

EXPANDED POLYSTYRENE TILES MISSING AND LOOSE

SOLUTION
Remove expanded polystyrene tiles

	3 x 3m	4 x 4m	8 x 4m
Prepare and apply emulsion paint to ceiling	270	370	740
Hang lining paper and emulsion paint	325	595	1190
Hang embossed paper and emulsion paint	370	640	1280

	Floors to Room Room Size		
	3 x 3m £	4 x 4m £	8 x 4m £

FLOOR IS BADLY STAINED/IN POOR DECORATIVE ORDER

SOLUTION
Redecorate flooring

	3 x 3m	4 x 4m	8 x 4m
Two coats matt finish polyurethane varnish to timber floors	295	425	845
Two coats non slip paint to concrete floors	295	425	845

	Rooms (wall height 2.75m) Room Size		
	3 x 3m 1 door 1 Window Size 1200 x 1200mm	4 x 4m 1 door 1 Window Size 1200 x 1200mm	8 x 4m 2 doors 2 Windows Sizes 900 x 1200mm and 1800 x 1800mm
	£	£	£

WALLS ARE BADLY STAINED/IN POOR DECORATIVE ORDER

SOLUTION
Clean existing walls

Remove mould from wall with fungicidal wash	370	410	600

Repaper walls

Hang woodchip or embossed paper and decorate	600	825	1210
Hang vinyl paper (PC £9 per roll)	800	1090	1600

Two coats emulsion paint

To existing painted and new plastered walls	310	400	475
To embossed paper or similar	380	425	615

Wash and clean down walls and apply two coats oil paint

To prepared plastered or embossed papered walls	375	510	745

	Walls 2.75m high			
---	3m long	4m long	5m long	8m long
	m²	m²	m²	m²
	8	11	14	22
	£	£	£	£

WALLS ARE BADLY STAINED/IN POOR DECORATIVE ORDER

SOLUTION
Clean existing walls

Remove mould from wall with fungicidal wash	**140**	**170**	**200**	**290**

Repaper walls

Hang woodchip or embossed paper	**185**	**225**	**265**	**385**
Hang woodchip or embossed paper and decorate	**260**	**330**	**400**	**610**
Hang vinyl paper (PC £9 per roll)	**275**	**360**	**440**	**685**

Two coats emulsion paint

To existing painted and new plastered walls	**125**	**150**	**170**	**240**
To embossed paper or similar	**140**	**170**	**200**	**290**

Wash and clean down walls and apply two coats oil paint

To prepared plastered or embossed papered walls	**160**	**195**	**230**	**335**

**DOORS ARE IN POOR
DECORATIVE ORDER**

SOLUTION
Prepare and redecorate doors

	Doors		Frames	
	One Side	Both Sides	One Side	Both Sides
	£	£	£	£
Clean down, one undercoat, one finishing coat oil paint	91	125	95	115
Clean down, one coat polyurethane varnish	76	94	88	105
Clean down, one coat woodstain system	98	140	125	140
Rub down, prepare and paint one coat knotting and primer, two undercoats, one finishing coat oil paint	120	180	125	160
Burn off paint, prepare and paint one coat knotting and primer, two undercoats, one finishing coat oil paint	140	230	160	205

	Door and Frame			
	Without Fanlight		With Fanlight	
	One Side	Both Sides	One Side	Both Sides
	£	£	£	£
Clean down, one undercoat, one finishing coat oil paint	130	185	140	200
Clean down, one coat polyurethane varnish	120	130	135	185
Clean down, one coat woodstain system	165	180	190	260
Rub down, prepare and paint one coat knotting and primer, two undercoats, one finishing coat oil paint	185	275	205	320
Burn off paint, prepare and paint one coat knotting and primer, two undercoats, one finishing coat oil paint	250	375	290	435

	Doors (number)			
	7	10	12	13
	£	£	£	£

DOORS ARE IN POOR DECORATIVE ORDER

SOLUTION
Prepare and redecorate doors one side

	7	10	12	13
Clean down, one undercoat, one finishing coat oil paint	290	320	380	415
Clean down, one coat polyurethane varnish	215	285	325	345
Clean down, one coat woodstain system	340	405	490	530
Rub down, prepare and paint one coat knotting and primer, two undercoats, one finishing coat oil paint	410	585	705	765
Burn off paint, prepare and paint one coat knotting and primer, two undercoats, one finishing coat oil paint	595	845	1020	1100

Prepare and redecorate doors both sides

	7	10	12	13
Clean down, one undercoat, one finishing coat oil paint	465	665	790	860
Clean down, one coat polyurethane varnish	310	440	530	575
Clean down, one coat woodstain system	565	810	965	1050
Rub down, prepare and paint one coat knotting and primer, two undercoats, one finishing coat oil paint	820	1170	1410	1530
Burn off paint, prepare and paint one coat knotting and primer, two undercoats, one finishing coat oil paint	1190	1690	2030	2190

	Doors (number)			
	7	10	12	13
	£	£	£	£

**DOOR FRAMES ARE IN POOR
DECORATIVE ORDER**

SOLUTION
Prepare and redecorate door frames one side

	7	10	12	13
Clean down, one undercoat, one finishing coat oil paint	260	370	440	475
Clean down, one coat polyurethane varnish	260	370	440	475
Clean down, one coat woodstain system	450	645	770	835
Rub down, prepare and paint one coat knotting and primer, two undercoats, one finishing coat oil paint	450	645	770	835
Burn off paint, prepare and paint one coat knotting and primer, two undercoats, one finishing coat oil paint	710	1010	1210	1310

Prepare and redecorate door frames both sides

	7	10	12	13
Clean down, one undercoat, one finishing coat oil paint	390	550	665	720
Clean down, one coat polyurethane varnish	390	550	665	720
Clean down, one coat woodstain system	580	825	990	1075
Rub down, prepare and paint one coat knotting and primer, two undercoats, one finishing coat oil paint	710	1010	1210	1310
Burn off paint, prepare and paint one coat knotting and primer, two undercoats, one finishing coat oil paint	1030	1470	1760	1910

	Doors and Frames (number)			
	7 £	10 £	12 £	13 £
		(without fanlights)		

DOOR AND FRAMES ARE IN POOR DECORATIVE ORDER

SOLUTION
Prepare and redecorate door and frames, one side

	7	10	12	13
Clean down, one undercoat, one finishing coat oil paint	490	700	840	910
Clean down, one coat polyurethane varnish	410	585	705	760
Clean down, one coat woodstain system	735	1050	1260	1430
Rub down, prepare and paint one coat knotting and primer, two undercoats, one finishing coat oil paint	860	1230	1480	1600
Burn off paint, prepare and paint one coat knotting and primer, two undercoats, one finishing coat oil paint	1300	1850	2220	2410

Prepare and redecorate door and frames, both sides

	7	10	12	13
Clean down, one undercoat, one finishing coat oil paint	850	1210	1450	1570
Clean down, one coat polyurethane varnish	690	990	1190	1290
Clean down, one coat woodstain system	1150	1630	1960	2120
Rub down, prepare and paint one coat knotting and primer, two undercoats, one finishing coat oil paint	1530	2180	2610	2830
Burn off paint, prepare and paint one coat knotting and primer, two undercoats, one finishing coat oil paint	2200	3150	3780	4100

	Doors and Frames (number)			
	7	10	12	13
	£	£	£	£

DOOR AND FRAMES ARE IN POOR DECORATIVE ORDER

(with fanlights)

SOLUTION

Prepare and redecorate door and frames, one side

	7	10	12	13
Clean down, one undercoat, one finishing coat oil paint	595	845	1020	1100
Clean down, one coat polyurethane varnish	515	735	880	955
Clean down, one coat woodstain system	915	1300	1560	1690
Rub down, prepare and paint one coat knotting and primer, two undercoats, one finishing coat oil paint	1050	1490	1780	1930
Burn off paint, prepare and paint one coat knotting and primer, two undercoats, one finishing coat oil paint	1580	2250	2700	2930

Prepare and redecorate door and frames, both sides

	7	10	12	13
Clean down, one undercoat, one finishing coat oil paint	1000	1430	1710	1860
Clean down, one coat polyurethane varnish	850	1210	1450	1570
Clean down, one coat woodstain system	1370	1960	2360	2560
Rub down, prepare and paint one coat knotting and primer, two undercoats, one finishing coat oil paint	1810	2590	3100	3360
Burn off paint, prepare and paint one coat knotting and primer, two undercoats, one finishing coat oil paint	2610	3740	4490	4860

	RANGE		
	Approx Window Size (mm)		
	600 x 900 £		1500 x 1200 £

WINDOWS ARE IN POOR DECORATIVE ORDER

SOLUTION
Prepare and redecorate windows

Clean down, one undercoat, one finishing coat oil paint

Windows with one pane	**74**	to	**90**
Windows with two or more panes	**77**	to	**95**
Georgian type windows with small panes	**84**	to	**125**

Clean down, one coat polyurethane varnish

Windows with one pane	**71**	to	**85**
Windows with two or more panes	**74**	to	**90**
Georgian type windows with small panes	**77**	to	**110**

Clean down, one coat woodstain system

Windows with one pane	**74**	to	**85**
Windows with two or more panes	**77**	to	**95**
Georgian type windows with small panes	**84**	to	**125**

Rub down, prepare and paint one coat knotting and primer, two undercoats, one finishing coat oil paint

Windows with one pane	**81**	to	**110**
Windows with two or more panes	**88**	to	**120**
Georgian type windows with small panes	**105**	to	**190**

Burn off paint, prepare and paint one coat knotting and primer, two undercoats, one finishing coat oil paint

Windows with one pane	**82**	to	**110**
Windows with two or more panes	**91**	to	**125**
Georgian type windows with small panes	**105**	to	**195**

SKIRTINGS ARE IN POOR DECORATIVE ORDER

	Skirting to Room (with one door opening) Room Size		
	3 x 3m £	4 x 4m £	8 x 4m £

SOLUTION
Prepare and redecorate skirtings

	3 x 3m £	4 x 4m £	8 x 4m £
Clean down, one undercoat, one finishing coat oil paint	155	190	260

	Skirting in Short Lengths		
	1m long £	2m long £	3m long £
Clean down, one undercoat, one finishing coat oil paint	85	92	99

	Wall String	Straight Flight Staircase Handrail	Balusters Posts & Base	Handrail etc Complete
	£	£	£	£

STAIRCASES ARE IN POOR DECORATIVE ORDER

SOLUTION
Prepare and redecorate staircases

Clean down, prepare and apply paint to wood surfaces

	Wall String	Handrail	Balusters Posts & Base	Handrail etc Complete
One undercoat and one finishing coat oil paint	90	110	220	295
One coat polyurethane varnish	90	82	185	235
One coat woodstain system	115	90	260	345
One undercoat and one finishing coat oil paint to balusters and one coat polyurethane varnish to handrails	90	82	220	270
One undercoat and one finishing coat oil paint to balusters and one coat woodstain to handrails	90	90	220	285

Rub down surfaces and apply paint to wood surfaces

	Wall String	Handrail	Balusters Posts & Base	Handrail etc Complete
One coat knotting and primer, two undercoats and one finishing coat oil paint	115	150	340	480
One coat knotting and primer, two undercoats and one finishing coat oil paint to balusters and one coat polyurethane varnish to handrails	115	82	250	330
One coat knotting and primer, two undercoats and one finishing coat oil paint to balusters and one coat woodstain to handrails	150	90	400	510

Burn off, prepare and apply paint to wood surfaces

	Wall String	Handrail	Balusters Posts & Base	Handrail etc Complete
One coat knotting and primer, two undercoats and one finishing coat oil paint	150	190	395	610
One coat knotting and primer, two undercoats and one finishing coat oil paint to balusters and one coat polyurethane varnish to handrails	150	82	395	505
One coat knotting and primer, two undercoats and one finishing coat oil paint to balusters and one coat woodstain to handrails	115	90	250	335

**RENDERED BOUNDARY WALL IS IN
POOR DECORATIVE ORDER**

SOLUTION
Redecorate boundary wall

	Length of Wall (m)			
	1	5	10	20
	£	£	£	£
One coat exterior cement paint or water compound or exterior Sandtex matt paint				
1m high	73	130	195	330
1.5m high	80	165	270	425
2m high	58	195	335	550

FENCES ARE IN POOR DECORATIVE ORDER

	Length of Fence (m)			
SOLUTION	1	5	10	20
Redecorate fences	£	£	£	£

Prepare timber and apply two coats of external quality wood treatment

1m high open boarded fencing	90	220	375	640
2m high open boarded fencing	125	375	640	1280
1m high close boarded fencing	87	200	340	565
2m high close boarded fencing	115	340	565	1130

Prepare timber and apply two coats of polyurethane varnish

1m high open boarded fencing	82	180	295	470
2m high open boarded fencing	105	295	470	940
1m high close boarded fencing	80	165	275	430
2m high close boarded fencing	105	275	430	855

Prepare timber and apply two coats of exterior quality gloss paint

1m high open boarded fencing	81	170	285	440
2m high open boarded fencing	105	285	440	885
1m high close boarded fencing	78	160	265	405
2m high close boarded fencing	99	265	405	815

Prepare metal surfaces and apply one coat primer and one coat gloss paint

1m high open boarded fencing	81	170	285	445
2m high open boarded fencing	105	285	445	890
1m high close boarded fencing	80	165	270	425
2m high close boarded fencing	105	270	425	845

GATES ARE IN POOR DECORATIVE ORDER

SOLUTION
Redecorate gates

	Gate Size		
	900 x 700mm	800 x 2000mm	900 x 2400mm
	£	£	£
Prepare timber and apply two coats of external quality wood treatment			
Open boarded gates	99	160	200
Close boarded gates	94	150	185
Prepare timber and apply two coats of polyurethane varnish			
Open boarded gates	88	135	180
Close boarded gates	87	130	155
Prepare timber and apply two coats of exterior quality gloss paint			
Open boarded gates	87	130	155
Close boarded gates	84	125	165
Prepare metal surfaces and apply one coat primer and one coat gloss paint			
Open boarded gates	87	130	155
Close boarded gates	87	130	155

VERTICAL CLADDING IS IN POOR DECORATIVE ORDER

SOLUTION
Prepare and redecorate timber cladding

	Height of Cladding (m)	Length of Cladding (m)		
		3 £	5 £	8 £
Clean down, one undercoat, one finishing coat oil paint	1.2	**120**	**160**	**220**
	3.0	**260**	**355**	**445**
Clean down, one coat polyurethane varnish	1.2	**98**	**125**	**165**
	3.0	**190**	**260**	**330**
Clean down, one coat woodstain system	1.2	**135**	**185**	**255**
	3.0	**305**	**425**	**540**
Rub down, prepare and paint one coat knotting and primer, two undercoats, one finishing coat oil paint	1.2	**165**	**235**	**340**
	3.0	**410**	**585**	**765**
Burn off paint, prepare and paint one coat knotting and primer, two undercoats, one finishing coat oil paint	1.2	**215**	**310**	**465**
	3.0	**505**	**740**	**975**

DOORS ARE IN POOR DECORATIVE ORDER

SOLUTION
Prepare and redecorate doors

		Doors	
		One Side	Both Sides
		£	£
Clean down, one undercoat, one finishing coat oil paint			
	flush or half glazed	90	125
	fully glazed	81	105
Clean down, one coat polyurethane varnish			
	flush or half glazed	78	98
	fully glazed	75	90
Clean down, one coat woodstain system			
	flush or half glazed	95	135
	fully glazed	77	95
Rub down, prepare and paint one coat knotting and primer, two undercoats, one finishing coat oil paint			
	flush or half glazed	125	190
	fully glazed	88	120
Burn off paint, prepare and paint one coat knotting and primer, two undercoats, one finishing coat oil paint			
	flush or half glazed	160	265
	fully glazed	155	250

DOOR FRAMES ARE IN POOR DECORATIVE ORDER

SOLUTION

	Door Frames	
	One Side	Both Sides
	£	£
Prepare and redecorate door frames		
Clean down, one undercoat, one finishing coat oil paint	110	165
Clean down, one coat polyurethane varnish	91	125
Clean down, one coat woodstain system	135	180
Rub down, prepare and paint one coat knotting and primer, two undercoats, one finishing coat oil paint	165	270
Burn off paint, prepare and paint one coat knotting and primer, two undercoats, one finishing coat oil paint	230	400

	Door and Frame			
	Without Fanlight		With Fanlight	
	One Side	Both Sides	One Side	Both Sides
	£	£	£	£

DOORS AND FRAMES ARE IN POOR DECORATIVE ORDER

SOLUTION
Prepare and redecorate doors
Clean down, one undercoat, one finishing coat oil paint

flush or half glazed doors	155	240	180	285
fully glazed doors	150	220	165	265

Clean down, one coat polyurethane varnish

flush or half glazed doors	120	170	135	190
fully glazed doors	115	165	130	190

Clean down, one coat woodstain system

flush or half glazed doors	160	260	185	300
fully glazed doors	140	220	165	265

Rub down, prepare and paint one coat knotting and primer, two undercoats, one finishing coat oil paint

flush or half glazed doors	250	415	290	500
fully glazed doors	215	345	255	430

Burn off paint, prepare and paint one coat knotting and primer, two undercoats, one finishing coat oil paint

flush or half glazed doors	365	630	435	770
fully glazed doors	355	615	415	750

	RANGE Approximate Window Size	
	600 x 900mm £	1500 x 1200mm £

WINDOWS ARE IN POOR DECORATIVE ORDER

SOLUTION
Prepare and redecorate windows

	One Side		
Clean down, one undercoat, one finishing coat oil paint	74	to	125
Clean down, one coat polyurethane varnish	71	to	110
Clean down, one coat woodstain system	74	to	125
Rub down, prepare and paint one coat knotting and primer, two undercoats, one finishing coat oil paint	81	to	190
Burn off paint, prepare and paint one coat knotting and primer, two undercoats, one finishing coat oil paint	82	to	195

	Both Sides		
Clean down, one undercoat, one finishing coat oil paint	88	to	205
Clean down, one coat polyurethane varnish	84	to	165
Clean down, one coat woodstain system	88	to	190
Rub down, prepare and paint one coat knotting and primer, two undercoats, one finishing coat oil paint	105	to	310
Burn off paint, prepare and paint one coat knotting and primer, two undercoats, one finishing coat oil paint	110	to	330

2:5 COMMON ALTERATION WORKS

EXTERIOR
Roof Coverings

	RANGE House Type		
	Terraced	Semi-Detached	Detached
	£	£	£
Replace roof covering including battens and felt			
Plain clay, concrete tiles	3950	8280	30170
Concrete interlocking tiles	2560	6320	18740
Clay pantiles	2760	7690	23260
Welsh blue natural slates	7300	14990	51460
Westmorland green natural slates	13210	27020	108840
Reconstructed stone slates	6510	13410	41800
Fibre cement slates	6910	12430	39830
Concrete interlocking slates	5910	12620	39630

	RANGE		
	House Type		
	Terraced	Semi-Detached	Detached
	£	£	£
Replace boarding to roof			
Replace softwood boarding			
Replace eaves fascia and soffit, including decoration			
ONE ELEVATION	480	825	1590
WHOLE HOUSE	960	2230	5090
Replace eaves fascia, including decoration			
ONE ELEVATION	275	450	825
WHOLE HOUSE	545	1220	2680
Replace eaves soffit, including decoration			
ONE ELEVATION	280	450	825
WHOLE HOUSE	555	1220	2680
Replace PVCu boarding			
Replace white eaves fascia and soffit			
ONE ELEVATION	510	735	1400
WHOLE HOUSE	1030	1930	4330
Replace white eaves fascia			
ONE ELEVATION	260	365	735
WHOLE HOUSE	520	990	2310
Replace white eaves soffit			
ONE ELEVATION	260	365	735
WHOLE HOUSE	520	990	2310
Replace mahogany eaves fascia and soffit			
ONE ELEVATION	640	930	1780
WHOLE HOUSE	1280	2490	5690
Replace mahogany eaves fascia			
ONE ELEVATION	360	525	1040
WHOLE HOUSE	720	1410	3280
Replace mahogany eaves soffit			
ONE ELEVATION	280	405	810
WHOLE HOUSE	555	1090	2550

Replace boarding to roof

Replace softwood boarding

Replace verges, including decoration

ONE SIDE ELEVATION			
One Side	**365**	to	**640**
Both sides	**730**	to	**1280**
TWO ELEVATIONS	**1260**	to	**2070**

Replace PVCu boarding

Replace verges with white PVCu

ONE SIDE ELEVATION			
One Side	**475**	to	**675**
Both sides	**950**	to	**1350**
TWO ELEVATIONS	**1620**	to	**2700**

Replace verges with mahogany PVCu

ONE SIDE ELEVATION			
One Side	**530**	to	**765**
Both sides	**1060**	to	**1530**
TWO ELEVATIONS	**1820**	to	**3050**

	RANGE House Type		
	Terraced	Semi-Detached	Detached
	£	£	£

Replace gutters and downpipes

PVCu

	Terraced	Semi-Detached	Detached
ONE ELEVATION	**420**	**495**	**735**
WHOLE HOUSE	**865**	**1440**	**2590**

Metal

	Terraced	Semi-Detached	Detached
ONE ELEVATION	**615**	**965**	**1710**
WHOLE HOUSE	**1260**	**2780**	**5950**

	RANGE		
	House Type		
	Terraced	Semi-Detached	Detached
	£	£	£
Replace windows			
Take out and install double glazed windows			
PVCu casement window	3820	7070	21140
PVCu sash window	11660	19400	62210
Take out and install windows including single glazing and decorating externally			
Timber casement window	3230	5780	16680
Metal casement window	3890	6890	20370
Timber double hung sash window	6780	11450	35720
Take out and install windows including double glazing and decorating externally			
Timber casement window	4680	8020	24060
Metal casement window	5090	8570	25910
Timber double hung sash window	7890	13160	41330
Replace windows and doors			
Take out and install double glazed windows and doors			
PVCu casement window	5670	8920	23000
PVCu sash window	13510	21260	64070
Take out and install windows and doors including single glazing and decorating externally			
Timber casement window	4980	7530	18730
Metal casement window	5630	8640	22420
Timber double hung sash window	8530	13190	37770
Take out and install windows and doors including double glazing and decorating externally			
Timber casement window	6430	9770	26110
Metal casement window	6840	10320	27960
Timber double hung sash window	9630	14910	43380

	Opening Width		
	3m	4m	5m
	£	£	£

Form opening between rooms and make good (excluding floor finish)

Form opening in non structural wall 440 530 620

Form opening in structural wall including providing steel beam over opening 865 1090 1320

	RANGE		
	House Type		
	Terraced	Semi-Detached	Detached
	£	£	£

Independent ceiling

Plasterboard on softwood battens and decorate
two coats of emulsion paint

	Terraced	Semi-Detached	Detached
GROUND FLOOR	825	1850	5860
FIRST FLOOR	1030	2040	6060
WHOLE HOUSE	1860	3890	11920

| | | RANGE | | |
| | | House Type | | |
		Terraced	Semi-Detached	Detached
		£	£	£

Timber floors

Replace flooring

Softwood floor boards

		Terraced	Semi-Detached	Detached
	GROUND FLOOR	**1550**	**3380**	**10060**
	FIRST FLOOR	**1260**	**3050**	**9730**
	WHOLE HOUSE	**2810**	**6430**	**19790**

| | Room Size | RANGE | | |
		Quality of Materials		
	m	£		£

Replace floor covering

Carpet

	Room Size			
	3 x 3	**655**	to	**845**
	4 x 4	**1160**	to	**1510**
	8 x 4	**2330**	to	**3010**

Carpet and underlay

	3 x 3	**740**	to	**930**
	4 x 4	**1310**	to	**1650**
	8 x 4	**2620**	to	**3310**

PVC flooring, sheeting or tiles

	3 x 3	**605**	to	**710**
	4 x 4	**1080**	to	**1260**
	8 x 4	**2160**	to	**2520**

Quarry tiles

	3 x 3	**990**		
	4 x 4	**1760**		
	8 x 4	**3520**		

Vitrified ceramic floor tiles

	3 x 3	**1370**		
	4 x 4	**2430**		
	8 x 4	**4870**		

Wood flooring

	3 x 3	**680**	to	**990**
	4 x 4	**1210**	to	**1760**
	8 x 4	**2410**	to	**3520**

	BATHROOM			SHOWER CUBICLE
		Tiling to		
	FULL HEIGHT	1200mm HIGH	600mm HIGH	FULL HEIGHT
	Area of Tiling			
	25m^2	11m^2	2m^2	10m^2
	£	£	£	£

Wall Tiling

Replace tiling

White glazed ceramic wall tiles	2290	1010	230	920
Light coloured glazed ceramic wall tiles	2440	1080	245	980
Dark coloured glazed ceramic wall tiles	2530	1120	265	1020

Bathroom size 2.5 x 2.5m x 2.75m high with one
door and one window size 600 x 600mm
Shower size 1.2 x 1.2 x 2.75m high with one door

	Single Items £
Fireplaces	
Replace pine mantle	375
Replace micro marble mantle	920
Replace hearth with Decostone	375
Replace hearth with conglomerate marble	440
Replace with conglomerate marble back panel and hearth, pine mantle	705
Replace with green marble or black granite back panel and hearth, stone micro marble mantle	2350
Remove fireplace, brick up opening including air brick and vent	255
Remove chimney breast	185

	Number of Doors	£	RANGE	£

Doors

Replace door, fix new ironmongery, decorate

Flush door

	Number of Doors	£		£
Flush door	1	295	to	515
	2	465	to	905
	5	1160	to	2260
	8	1860	to	3620
Six panel door	1	495	to	845
	2	870	to	1570
	5	2170	to	3910
	8	3470	to	6250

	Cable Length to Existing (m)	Fittings (number)		
		1 £	2 £	5 £
New power sockets				
New surface mounted single socket outlet with PVCu conduit	1	105	140	250
	2	145	185	290
	5	195	230	340
New surface mounted double socket outlet with PVCu conduit	1	125	175	340
	2	165	220	385
	5	215	270	430
New flush mounted single socket outlet including cutting chase	1	115	160	285
	2	160	210	355
	5	210	255	400
New flush mounted double socket outlet including cutting chase	1	130	195	395
	2	175	245	445
	5	225	290	490
New light points				
New surface mounted ceiling rose, pendant and wall switch with PVCu conduit	4	190	245	410
	5	215	270	435
	6	240	290	455
New surface mounted ceiling lampholder and pull switch with PVCu conduit	1	130	165	275
	2	155	190	300
	5	220	255	365
New flush mounted ceiling rose, pendant and wall switch, cutting chase	4	170	225	390
	5	185	240	400
	6	195	250	415
New flush mounted ceiling lampholder and pull switch, cutting chase	1	115	155	260
	2	130	165	275
	5	165	200	310

New Sanitary suites

	Suites £
Bathroom	
Basin and pressed steel bath	**1380**
Basin and plastic bath	**1540**
Low level cistern WC with seat, basin and pressed steel bath	**2100**
Low level cistern WC with seat, basin and plastic bath	**2260**
Shower Room	
Low level cistern WC with seat, basin and plastic shower tray	**1720**
Low level cistern WC with seat, basin and ceramic shower tray	**1870**
Cloakroom	
Low level cistern WC with seat and basin	**1240**
Kitchen	
Stainless steel sink with single bowl and drainer	**575**
Belfast sink	**710**

	RANGE		
	£		£
Replace heating system excluding pipework			
Wall mounted boiler, single and double panel radiators wall thermostat and programmer			
Clockwork programmer	**4420**	to	**6980**
Digital programmer	**5150**	to	**7710**
Replace heating system including pipework			
Wall mounted boiler, single and double panel radiators, pipework, wall thermostat and programmer			
Clockwork programmer	**6410**	to	**10510**
Digital programmer	**7140**	to	**11240**

	Length of Pipe Run (m)			
	5	10	15	20
	£	£	£	£

Install new drain runs for new sanitary fittings

100mm pipe

Excavate through soft surface, average excavation depth 1000mm deep, replace pipe, make good ground

	5	10	15	20
Excavate through soft surface... make good ground	**640**	**1220**	**1800**	**2380**
Excavate through concrete or paving or tarmac surface, average excavation depth 1000mm deep, replace pipe, make good surface to match existing.	**870**	**1760**	**2650**	**3540**

	Single Items £
Form new manholes	
Excavate pit, concrete base, engineering brick sides, concrete cover slab with cast iron cover and frame, concrete benching and vitrified clay channel bends	
600 x 450 x 750mm deep internally	**470**
600 x 450 x 1000mm deep internally	**605**

2:6 TOTAL PROJECT COSTS

HOUSE EXTENSIONS

NOTE:
The works in this section generally **exclude** any
floor finishes.

	Floor Size m	£	RANGE	£

HOUSE EXTENSIONS
Excludes forming openings to existing building

Single Storey with one window

	Floor Size m	£		£
	3 x 3	**17000**	to	**21000**
	3 x 5	**21500**	to	**26500**
	4 x 4	**22500**	to	**28000**
	4 x 6	**30000**	to	**36000**

Two Storey with two windows

	Floor Size m	£		£
	3 x 3	**28000**	to	**36500**
	3 x 5	**35500**	to	**44000**
	4 x 4	**38000**	to	**47500**
	4 x 6	**49000**	to	**61000**

Single storey flat roof

Single storey pitched roof

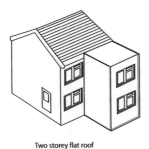

Two storey flat roof

Two storey pitched roof

	Floor Size m	£	RANGE	£
CONSERVATORIES				
Including radiator				
	3 x 3	**10000**	to	**12500**
	4 x 4	**16000**	to	**21000**
	4 x 6	**23000**	to	**30500**
Including forming opening in existing external cavity wall and new pair of glazed doors, radiator				
	3 x 3	**12500**	to	**14500**
	4 x 4	**18500**	to	**23000**
	4 x 6	**25500**	to	**33000**
GARDEN ROOMS				
Similar to conservatories but with solid roof Including radiator				
	3 x 3	**10500**	to	**13000**
	4 x 4	**17000**	to	**22000**
	4 x 6	**24500**	to	**32000**
Including forming opening in existing external cavity wall and new pair of glazed doors, radiator				
	3 x 3	**13000**	to	**15500**
	4 x 4	**19500**	to	**24500**
	4 x 6	**27000**	to	**34000**

Floor Size m	RANGE £		£

LOFT CONVERSIONS

Comprising clearing loft, relocating existing tanks, insulation, softwood framing and plasterboard to walls, insulation and plasterboard to ceiling, softwood floor, new straight flight staircase, new electrics and heating, openings in roof for windows.

	Floor Size m	2 Windows £		4 Windows £
With Velux or similar windows				
	4 x 5	**16000**	to	**21000**
	6 x 5	**17000**	to	**22000**
	12 x 7	**25500**	to	**30500**
With dormer windows				
	4 x 5	**27000**	to	**44000**
	6 x 5	**28000**	to	**45000**
	12 x 7	**38000**	to	**54000**

Velux Windows

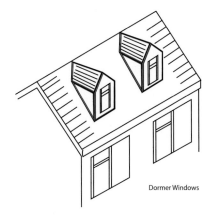

Dormer Windows

BASEMENT CONVERSIONS

	RANGE		
	Floor Size		
	3 x 3m	3 x 5m	4 x 6m
	£	£	£

BASEMENT CONVERSIONS

	3 x 3m £	3 x 5m £	4 x 6m £
Replace door and frame and staircase, plaster and paint walls and ceilings, screed floor, install skirting and decorate	**8500**	**10000**	**11500**
As above and including tanking walls and floor	**18500**	**24500**	**29500**

PORCHES

	750mm deep x		
	1200mm	1950mm	3000mm
	£	£	£
Canopies			
Softwood frame and fascia, plywood soffit, plain tile roof, lead flashings, decoration	**635**	**1030**	**1640**
GRP canopy with tile effect roof	**415**	**540**	**820**

	RANGE		
	Quality of Material		
	£		£

Enclosed porches
Purpose built PVCu on concrete base

		£		£
	2 x 1	**3400**	to	**8600**
	3 x 2.5	**5900**	to	**12000**

Brick and timber or PVCu doors and windows

		£		£
	2 x 1	**5500**	to	**7500**
	3 x 2.5	**10500**	to	**13000**

		RANGE		
		Quality of Materials		
		£		£

GARAGES
Brick with flat roof
Single width	6 x 3	**11500**	to	**18500**
Double width	6 x 5	**15500**	to	**24500**

Brick with pitched roof
Single width	6 x 3	**12500**	to	**21000**
Double width	6 x 5	**16000**	to	**27000**

Purpose built, precast concrete
Single width	5 x 3	**3200**	to	**5200**
Double width	5 x 5	**5200**	to	**8900**

		Without New Base		With New Concrete Base
		£		£

CAR PORTS
Installing on existing hardstanding or providing
new concrete hardstanding

Single width	2.6 x 3m	**1400**	to	**2500**
Double width	4 x 3.5m	**2500**	to	**4500**
Cantilever canopy	2.4 x 3.2m	**3400**	to	**5500**

	RANGE Quality of Materials		
	£		£

KITCHENS

Remove existing and install new units, fittings, flooring, wall tiling and decoration

Size Range
  Terraced 8m^2 Detached 24m^2
Quality Range
  From: Standard DIY Superstore fittings and
    vinyl floors
  To: Bespoke fittings and ceramic floor
    tiling

	£		£
TERRACED	**13500**	to	**24000**
SEMI DETACHED	**17000**	to	**26000**
DETACHED	**38000**	to	**125000**

BATHROOMS

Remove existing and install new sanitary fittings, flooring, wall tiling and decoration

Size Range
  Terraced 6m^2 Detached 16m^2
Quality Range
  From: Standard DIY Superstore fittings and
    vinyl floors
  To: Bespoke fittings and ceramic floor
    tiling

	£		£
TERRACED	**5000**	to	**10500**
SEMI DETACHED	**7000**	to	**12500**
DETACHED	**7500**	to	**42000**

2:7 Weather Damage

STORM DAMAGE
Light Damage

REPLACE MISSING/ BROKEN TILES/ SLATES

	Number of Tiles/Slates in One Location			
	1	2	5	6
SOLUTION	£	£	£	£
Replace tile	285	305	325	335
Replace slate	290	315	340	355

RESECURE LOOSE TILES/ SLATES

	1	2	5	6
SOLUTION				
Resecure tile or slates	280	290	305	310

EAVES OR VERGE BOARDING IS LOOSE

		RANGE	
	£		£
Resecure eaves fascia, including decoration	230	to	420
Resecure eaves soffit, including decoration			
ONE ELEVATION	240	to	445
Resecure eaves fascia and soffit, including decoration			
ONE ELEVATION	335	to	725
Resecure verge boarding, including decoration			
ONE SIDE	280	to	350

GUTTERS/ RAINWATER PIPES ARE MISSING

	Length of Gutter/Pipe (m)		
	1	2	3
SOLUTION	£	£	£
Replace gutters			
PVCu	140	180	215
Aluminium	155	210	265
Cast iron, including decoration	190	280	365
Replace pipes			
PVCu	130	160	190
Aluminium	160	215	275
Cast iron, including decoration	205	305	405

GUTTERS/ RAINWATER FITTINGS ARE MISSING

	Fittings (number)		
	1	2	3
	£	£	£
SOLUTION			
Replace PVCu balloon grating	71	79	88
Replace PVCu gutter brackets	71	79	88

REFIX LOOSE TV AERIAL

	Single Items
	£
SOLUTION	
Refix aerial to chimney stack, including renewing fixings	**215**

VERTICAL TILING IS DAMAGED OR MISSING

	Tiles in One Location (number)		
	1	5	10
SOLUTION	£	£	£
Replace tiles or slates at low level			
Replace vertical tiles	**125**	**180**	**240**
Replace vertical slates	**130**	**205**	**280**
Replace tiles or slates at high level			
Replace vertical tiles	**160**	**215**	**280**
Replace vertical slates			
	165	**235**	**325**

WINDOW PANE IS BROKEN

	RANGE		
	Approx Pane Size (mm)		
	300 x 600		900 x 900
	£		£
SOLUTION			
Remove glass and putty, prepare and reglaze	**110**	to	**225**

BRANCHES HAVE SPLIT

	Branches (number)			
SOLUTION	1	2	3	5
Prune branches	£	£	£	£
Pruning small branches not exceeding 1m long	**60**	**61**	**67**	**93**
Pruning large branches exceeding 1m long	**61**	**64**	**76**	**135**

BOUNDARY WALL HAS BEEN DAMAGED

SOLUTION
Re-build freestanding brick wall 1m high

	Length of Wall (m)			
	1	2	3	5
	£	£	£	£
Half brick thick wall 1m high	**185**	**310**	**440**	**635**
One brick thick wall 1m high	**300**	**490**	**730**	**1220**

FENCE PANELS OR POSTS ARE MISSING OR DAMAGED

	Panels or Posts (number)			
	1	2	3	5
	£	£	£	£

SOLUTION
Replace fence or post
Replace interwoven or timber lap fencing
2m long panel and capping

	1	2	3	5
1m high	110	155	210	295
2m high	130	195	265	405
Replace intermediate post 2m long overall				
Softwood	79	105	125	170
Oak	84	115	140	190
Concrete	95	135	175	250

GATES ARE MISSING OR DAMAGED

SOLUTION
Replace gate

	Single Items £
Ledged and braced matchboard gate, including ironmongery	470
Framed, ledged and braced matchboard gate, including ironmongery	560
Single gate and posts, decorated, including stops and ironmongery	255
Double gates and posts, decorated, including ironmongery and stops, centre stop set in concrete	435

REPLACE MISSING/BROKEN TILES/SLATES

SOLUTION	Tiles/Slates in One Location (m²)			
	1	2	5	6
	£	£	£	£
Plain clay tile	355	455	485	590
Concrete interlocking tile	305	355	495	545
Natural slate	420	580	795	955

REPAIR SMALL PATCHES IN TOP LAYER OF FELT ROOF

SOLUTION	Repairs (number)		
	1	2	5
	£	£	£
Cutting out defective layer, rebonding to adjacent layers and covering with single layer felt			
Small patches not exceeding 0.5m²	250	280	355
0.5 - 2m²	265	310	445
2 - 5m²	315	410	700

REPLACE MISSING OR DAMAGED POTS

SOLUTION	Pots per Stack		
	1	2	4
Replace pots and flaunching	£	£	£
450mm high pot	760	930	1260
900mm high pot	960	1330	2060

REPLACE MISSING OR DAMAGED GUTTERS AND DOWNPIPES

SOLUTION	House Type		
	Terraced	Semi-Detached	Detached
	£	£	£
Replace gutters and downpipes to one elevation			
PVCu	420	495	735
Metal	615	965	1710

VERTICAL SHIPLAP CLADDING IS DAMAGED

SOLUTION	Individual Board (number)	Area (m^2)		
		2	3	5
	£	£	£	£
Replace shiplap cladding at low level	**100**	**245**	**330**	**500**
Replace shiplap cladding at high level	**165**	**285**	**370**	**540**

VERTICAL TILING IS DAMAGED OR MISSING

SOLUTION	Area (m^2)			
	2	3	5	6
	£	£	£	£
Replace tiles or slates at low level				
Replace vertical tiles	**310**	**425**	**650**	**765**
Replace vertical slates	**475**	**720**	**1210**	**1470**
Replace tiles or slates at high level				
Replace vertical tiles	**355**	**470**	**700**	**810**
Replace vertical slates	**520**	**765**	**1260**	**1500**

ENTRANCE CANOPY IS DAMAGED OR MISSING

SOLUTION	Canopy Area 750mm x		
	1200mm	1950mm	3000mm
	£	£	£
Softwood framed canopy with roof tiles on plywood	**615**	**990**	**1580**
GRP canopy with tile effect roof	**400**	**510**	**790**

TREES HAVE MOVED AND ARE DANGEROUS TO STRUCTURE

SOLUTION	Single
Remove trees	Items
	£
Cut down and remove small trees and shrubs	**435**
Cut down and remove large trees	**1050**

BOUNDARY WALL HAS BEEN DAMAGED

	Length of Wall (m)			
SOLUTION	1	2	3	5
Re-build freestanding brick wall	£	£	£	£
Half brick thick wall				
1.5m high	**255**	**445**	**585**	**970**
2m high	**310**	**515**	**765**	**1280**
One brick thick wall				
1.5m high	**425**	**730**	**1100**	**1830**
2m high	**490**	**980**	**1460**	**2440**

FENCING IS MISSING OR DAMAGED

SOLUTION	Length of Fence (m)			
Replace fence	1	5	10	20
	£	£	£	£
Replace chestnut pale fencing, softwood posts 1000mm high with 2 or 3 wires	**165**	**515**	**1030**	**2050**
Close boarded fencing				
Softwood posts	**170**	**540**	**1085**	**2170**
Oak posts	**180**	**605**	**1210**	**2420**
Reinforced concrete posts	**195**	**685**	**1370**	**2740**
Interwoven panel fencing				
Softwood posts	**170**	**540**	**1090**	**2170**
Oak posts	**185**	**640**	**1280**	**2560**
Reinforced concrete slotted posts	**205**	**725**	**1450**	**2900**

REPLACE PITCHED ROOF COVERING INCLUDING BATTENS AND FELT

	RANGE		
		House Type	
SOLUTION	Terraced	Semi-Detached	Detached
	£	£	£
Plain clay, concrete tiles	3950	8280	30170
Concrete interlocking tiles	2560	6320	18740
Clay pantiles	2760	7690	23260
Welsh blue natural slates	7300	14990	51460
Westmorland green natural slates	13210	27020	108840
Reconstructed stone slates	6510	13410	41800
Fibre cement slates	6910	12430	39830
Concrete interlocking slates	5910	12620	39630

REPLACE FLAT ROOF COVERING

	Area (m^2)		
	10	15	25
SOLUTION	£	£	£
Three layer felt, boarding and insulation	1810	2700	4450

REBUILD CHIMNEY STACK

SOLUTION	Pots per Stack	RANGE		
		£		£
Rebuild stack 1m high, replace pots	1	2370	to	2970
	2	3360	to	4150
	4	5130	to	5930
Rebuild stack 2m high, replace pots	1	3150	to	3950
	2	4740	to	5930
	4	5930	to	7300

REBUILD WALL DAMAGED BY STORM OR TREE

SOLUTION	ELEVATION	RANGE House Type		
		Terraced	Semi-Detached	Detached
		£	£	£
Rebuild wall including insulation	Front or Rear	**12590**	**29500**	**45180**
Rebuild wall including insulation	Side	**41420**		**43610**

DRIVEWAY HAS BROKEN UP, DUE TO UPROOTING OF TREE

SOLUTION	Length of Drive (m)	
Replace driveway	5	10
	£	£
Replace single width driveway		
75mm two coat rolled bitumen macadam	**720**	**1440**
Precast concrete slabs, 600 x 600	**865**	**1730**
Precast concrete coloured blocks, 200 x 100	**1510**	**3020**
Clay brick paviours 75mm thick (PC £40/100)	**1580**	**3160**
Clay brick paviours 25mm thick (PC £30/100)	**1460**	**2920**
Crazy paving; broken precast concrete paving slabs	**1510**	**3020**
100mm thick insitu concrete with formwork to edges, to falls, tamped finish and trowelled edge	**1060**	**2120**

FOOTPATH HAS BROKEN UP, DUE TO UPROOTING OF TREE

SOLUTION	Length of Footpath (m)	
Replace footpath	5	10
	£	£
Replace footpath 1.2m wide		
75mm two coat rolled bitumen macadam	**350**	**580**
Precast concrete slabs, 600 x 600 x 50mm	**435**	**690**
Precast concrete coloured blocks, 200 x 100	**610**	**1220**
Clay brick paviours 75mm thick (PC £40/100)	**635**	**1270**
Clay brick paviours 25mm thick (PC £30/100)	**585**	**1170**
Crazy paving; broken precast concrete paving slabs	**605**	**1210**
75mm thick insitu concrete with formwork to edges, to falls, tamped finish and trowelled edge	**405**	**810**

	Area (m²)			
BRICKWORK/RENDERING IS STAINED	1	2	5	10
IN SMALL AREAS	£	£	£	£

SOLUTION
Clean with water and brush lightly to walls

	87	115	200	340

BRANCHES HAVE SPLIT

SOLUTION
Prune branches

	Branches (number)			
	1	2	3	5
	£	£	£	£
Pruning small branches not exceeding 1m long	60	61	67	93
Pruning large branches exceeding 1m long	61	64	76	135

BOUNDARY WALL HAS BEEN DAMAGED

SOLUTION
Re-build freestanding brick wall

	Length of Wall (m)			
	1	2	3	5
	£	£	£	£
Half brick thick wall 1m high	185	310	440	635
One brick thick wall 1m high	300	490	730	1220

FENCE PANELS OR POSTS ARE MISSING OR DAMAGED

SOLUTION
Replace fencing

	Panels or Posts (number)			
	1	2	3	5
	£	£	£	£
Replace interwoven or timber lap fencing 2m long panel and capping				
1m high	110	155	205	295
2m high	130	195	265	405
Replace intermediate post 2m long overall				
Softwood	79	105	125	170
Oak	84	115	140	190
Concrete	95	135	175	250

GATES ARE MISSING OR DAMAGED

SOLUTION
Replace gates and posts

	Single Items £
Ledged and braced matchboard gate, including ironmongery	470
Framed, ledged and braced matchboard gate, including ironmongery	560
Single gate and posts, decorated, including stops and ironmongery	255
Double gates and posts, decorated, including ironmongery and stops, centre stop set in concrete	435

	RANGE House Type		
EXTERNAL BRICKWORK/RENDERING IS STAINED IN PATCHES	Terraced	Semi-Detached	Detached
	£	£	£

SOLUTION

| Clean with water and brush lightly to walls 1.5m high | 845 | 2590 | 4620 |

	Area of Flooring (m^2)			
	1	2	3	5
FLOOR BOARDS ARE DAMAGED	£	£	£	£

SOLUTION

Replace softwood floor boarding				
	190	270	370	570

FLOOR COVERING IS DAMAGED IN SMALL AREAS

SOLUTION

Replace floor covering in damaged areas

	Patches not Exceeding 0.5m^2 (number)			
	1	2	3	5
	£	£	£	£
PVC floor tiles	77	93	110	140
Wood strip flooring	105	145	185	265
Wood block flooring	120	180	235	350

PLASTER IS DAMAGED IN SMALL AREAS

SOLUTION
Replaster patches to wall plaster

	Number of Patches (number)	RANGE Quality of Materials		
		£		£
Replaster walls, patches not exceeding 1m² area	1	**135**	to	**175**
	2	**205**	to	**290**
	3	**275**	to	**400**
	5	**420**	to	**625**

CRACKS HAVE APPEARED IN PLASTER

SOLUTION
Repair cracks

	Length of crack (m)			
	1	2	3	5
	£	£	£	£
Rake out and refill crack in plaster	**67**	**74**	**81**	**93**

REDECORATE WALLS INCLUDING SKIRTING

SOLUTION
Clean existing walls, remove mould with fungicidal wash

	Rooms (wall height 2.75m) Room Size		
	3 x 3m	4 x 4m	8 x 4m
	£	£	£
	370	**410**	**600**

	Length of Cable (m)			
	1	2	3	5
WIRING HAS BEEN DAMAGED	£	£	£	£

SOLUTION

Renew power cable	**56**	**68**	**80**	**105**

	Fittings (number)			
	1	2	3	5
FITTINGS HAVE BEEN DAMAGED	£	£	£	£

SOLUTION

Replace surface mounted socket outlet	**79**	**115**	**155**	**225**
Replace flush mounted socket outlet and box	**87**	**135**	**175**	**260**

TREES HAVE MOVED AND ARE DANGEROUS TO STRUCTURE

SOLUTION

	Single Items £
Remove trees	
Cut down and remove small trees and shrubs	**435**
Cut down and remove large trees	**1050**

BOUNDARY WALL HAS BEEN DAMAGED

SOLUTION

Re-build freestanding brick wall

	Length of wall (m)			
	1	2	3	5
	£	£	£	£
Half brick thick wall				
1.5m high	**255**	**445**	**585**	**970**
2m high	**310**	**515**	**765**	**1280**
One brick thick wall				
1.5m high	**425**	**730**	**1100**	**1830**
2m high	**490**	**980**	**1460**	**2438**

FENCING IS DAMAGED OR MISSING

SOLUTION

Replace fencing

	1 £	5 £	10 £	20 £
		Length of Fence (m)		
Replace galvanised chain link fencing, with reinforced concrete posts				
900mm high	170	560	1120	2240
1200mm high	180	610	1220	2440
Replace galvanised chain link fencing to existing posts				
900mm high	80	175	295	475
1200mm high	85	185	310	510
Replace chestnut pale fencing, softwood posts				
1000mm high with 2 or 3 wires	165	515	1030	2050
Close boarded fencing				
Softwood posts	170	540	1090	2170
Oak posts	180	605	1210	2420
Reinforced concrete posts	195	685	1370	2740
Interwoven panel fencing				
Softwood posts	170	540	1085	2165
Oak posts	185	640	1280	2560
Reinforced concrete slotted posts	205	725	1450	2900

EXTERNAL BRICKWORK/RENDERING IS STAINED

	RANGE House Type		
	Terraced	Semi-Detached	Detached
	£	£	£

SOLUTION

	Terraced	Semi-Detached	Detached
Clean with water and brush lightly to walls 1.5m high	845	2590	4620
Prepare and one coat exterior cement paint to existing rendered elevations	1245	3400	6420
Prepare and one coat waterproof compound to existing rendered elevations	1180	3140	6010

HOUSE HAS BEEN FLOODED INSIDE

	RANGE House Type		
	Terraced	Semi-Detached	Detached
	£	£	£

SOLUTION

	Terraced	Semi-Detached	Detached
Dry house including heating and disinfecting	945	1890	5610

FLOOR BOARDS ARE DAMAGED

SOLUTION
Replace floorboards

	RANGE House Type		
	Terraced	Semi Detached	Detached
	£	£	£
Replace softwood floor boards	**1550**	**3380**	**10060**

	Floors to Room Room Size		
	3 x 3m	4 x 4m	8 x 4m
	£	£	£
Replace softwood floor boards	**890**	**1300**	**2580**

FLOOR JOISTS ARE DAMAGED

SOLUTION
Replace joist

	Length of timber (m)			
	1	2	3	5
Replace 50 x 150mm floor joist	£	£	£	£
Take up floor boards, renew joists, refix boards	**110**	**160**	**210**	**305**
Take up floor boards, renew joists, lay new softwood boarded floor	**205**	**340**	**480**	**680**

FLOOR COVERING IS DAMAGED

SOLUTION

Replace floor covering	Room size m	RANGE Quality of Materials £		£
Replace carpet and underlay	3 x 3	**740**	to	**930**
	4 x 4	**1305**	to	**1650**
	8 x 4	**2620**	to	**3300**
Replace PVC flooring, sheeting or tiles	3 x 3	**605**	to	**710**
	4 x 4	**1130**	to	**1320**
	8 x 4	**2160**	to	**2520**
Replace wood flooring	3 x 3	**680**	to	**990**
	4 x 4	**1210**	to	**1760**
	8 x 4	**2410**	to	**3530**

INTERNAL DOORS ARE DAMAGED

SOLUTION

	RANGE Quality of Material per door £		£
Remove door, hang new door including refixing ironmongery, decorate	**245**	to	**400**

SKIRTINGS ARE DAMAGED

SOLUTION

Replace softwood skirting	Room Size	RANGE Quality/size of Materials £		£
	3 x 3m	**340**	to	**360**
	4 x 4m	**460**	to	**490**
	8 x 4m	**705**	to	**745**

PLASTER IS DAMAGED

	Room Size	RANGE Quality of Materials		
		£		£

SOLUTION

Replaster walls	3 x 3m	1345	to	2610
	4 x 4m	1850	to	3570
	8 x 4m	2690	to	5230

REDECORATE WALLS INCLUDING SKIRTING

	Rooms (wall height 2.75m) Room Size		
	3 x 3m	4 x 4m	8 x 4m
	£	£	£

SOLUTION

	3 x 3m	4 x 4m	8 x 4m
Clean existing walls, remove mould with fungicidal wash	370	410	600
Repaper walls with vinyl paper and repaint skirtings	960	1280	1825
Emulsion paint to walls and repaint skirtings	470	585	710

REPLACE WIRING AND POWER POINTS
TO GROUND FLOOR DAMAGED BY FLOODING

	RANGE House Type		
	Terraced	Semi-Detached	Detached
	£	£	£

SOLUTION

	Terraced	Semi-Detached	Detached
Complete rewire to concealed power circuits	1070	1440	1980

CLEAN OUT CENTRAL HEATING SYSTEM

	Single Item
	£

SOLUTION

Power flush system	435

REBUILD WALL DAMAGED BY FLOODING OR TREE

SOLUTION
Rebuild wall

	ELEVATION	Terraced £	RANGE House Type Semi-Detached	Detached £
Rebuild wall including insulation	Front or Rear	**12590**	**29500**	**45180**

	ELEVATION	Semi-Detached £		Detached £
Rebuild wall including insulation	Side	**41420**	to	**43610**

DRIVEWAY HAS BROKEN UP, DUE TO FLOODING/UPROOTING OF TREE

SOLUTION
Replace driveway

	Length of Drive (m) 5 £	10 £
Replace single width driveway		
75mm two coat rolled Bitumen macadam	**720**	**1440**
Precast concrete slabs, 600 x 600 x 50mm	**865**	**1725**
Precast concrete blocks, 200 x 100 x 60mm, coloured	**1510**	**3020**
Clay brick paviours 75mm thick (PC £40/100)	**1575**	**3160**
Clay brick paviours 25mm thick (PC £30/100)	**1460**	**2930**
Crazy paving of broken precast concrete paving slabs	**1510**	**3020**
100mm thick insitu concrete with formwork to edges, to falls, tamped finish and trowelled edge	**1060**	**2110**
Replace double width driveway		
75mm two coat rolled Bitumen macadam	**1440**	**2880**
Precast concrete slabs, 600 x 600 x 50mm	**1730**	**3450**
Precast concrete blocks, 200 x 100 x 60mm, coloured	**3010**	**6010**
Clay brick paviours 75mm thick (PC £40/100)	**3160**	**6310**
Clay brick paviours 25mm thick (PC £30/100)	**2910**	**5820**
Crazy paving of broken precast concrete paving slabs	**3030**	**6050**
100mm thick insitu concrete with formwork to edges, to falls, tamped finish and trowelled edge	**2110**	**4210**

**FOOTPATH HAS BROKEN UP, DUE TO
UPROOTING OF TREE**

	Length of Footpath (m)	
	5	10
SOLUTION	£	£
Replace footpath		
Replace footpath 1.2m wide		
75mm two coat rolled Bitumen macadam	**345**	**575**
Precast concrete slabs, 600 x 600 x 50mm	**435**	**690**
Precast concrete blocks, 200 x 100 x 60mm, coloured	**605**	**1210**
Clay brick paviours 75mm thick (PC £40/100)	**635**	**1270**
Clay brick paviours 25mm thick (PC £30/100)	**585**	**1170**
Crazy paving of broken precast concrete paving slabs	**605**	**1210**
75mm thick insitu concrete with formwork to edges, to falls, tamped finish and trowelled edge	**405**	**805**

GUTTERS ARE MISSING/DAMAGED

Length of Gutter/Pipe (m)

	1	2	3
SOLUTION	£	£	£
Replace gutters			
PVCu	**140**	**180**	**215**
Aluminium	**155**	**210**	**270**
Cast iron, including decoration	**190**	**280**	**365**

GUTTERS/ RAINWATER FITTINGS ARE MISSING

Fittings (number)

	1	2	3
SOLUTION	£	£	£
Replace PVCu balloon grating	**71**	**79**	**88**
Replace PVCu gutter brackets	**71**	**79**	**88**

ENTRANCE CANOPY IS MISSING OR DAMAGED

	Canopy Area 750mm x		
	1200mm	1950mm	3000mm
SOLUTION	£	£	£
Softwood framed canopy with roof tiles on plywood	**615**	**990**	**1580**
GRP canopy with tile effect roof	**400**	**510**	**790**

BRANCHES HAVE SPLIT

SOLUTION	Branches (number)			
	1	2	3	5
Prune trees	£	£	£	£
Pruning small branches not exceeding 1m long	**60**	**61**	**67**	**93**
Pruning large branches exceeding 1m long	**61**	**64**	**76**	**135**

BOUNDARY WALL HAS BEEN DAMAGED

SOLUTION	Length of Wall (m)			
	1	2	3	5
Re-build freestanding brick wall	£	£	£	£
Half brick thick wall 1m high	**185**	**310**	**440**	**635**
One brick thick wall 1m high	**300**	**490**	**730**	**1220**

FENCE PANELS OR POSTS ARE DAMAGED

SOLUTION
Replace fence or post

	Panels or Posts (number)			
	1	2	3	5
	£	£	£	£
Replace interwoven or timber lap fencing 2m long panel and capping				
1m high	**110**	**155**	**205**	**295**
2m high	**130**	**195**	**265**	**405**
Replace intermediate post 2m long overall				
Softwood	**79**	**105**	**125**	**170**
Oak	**84**	**115**	**140**	**190**
Concrete	**95**	**135**	**175**	**250**

TREES HAVE MOVED AND ARE DANGEROUS TO STRUCTURE

SOLUTION Remove trees	Single Items £
Cut down and remove small trees and shrubs	**435**
Cut down and remove large trees	**1050**

SURFACE OF DRIVEWAY HAS BROKEN UP, DUE TO SALT SNOW CLEARING DAMAGE

SOLUTION Replace driveway	Length of Drive (m)	
	5 £	10 £
Replace single width driveway		
75mm two coat rolled Bitumen macadam	**720**	**1440**
Precast concrete slabs, 600 x 600 x 50mm	**865**	**1725**
Crazy paving of broken precast concrete paving slabs	**1510**	**3020**
100mm thick insitu concrete with formwork to edges, to falls, tamped finish and trowelled edge	**1060**	**2110**
Replace double width driveway		
75mm two coat rolled Bitumen macadam	**1440**	**2880**
Precast concrete slabs, 600 x 600 x 50mm	**1730**	**3450**
Crazy paving of broken precast concrete paving slabs	**3030**	**6050**
100mm thick insitu concrete with formwork to edges, to falls, tamped finish and trowelled edge	**2110**	**4210**

FOOTPATH HAS BROKEN UP, DUE TO DAMAGE BY SALT AND SNOW CLEARING

	Length of Footpath (m)	
SOLUTION	5	10
Replace footpath	£	£

Replace footpath 1.2m wide

75mm two coat rolled Bitumen macadam	**345**	**575**
Precast concrete slabs, 600 x 600 x 50mm	**435**	**690**
Crazy paving of broken precast concrete paving slabs	**605**	**1210**
75mm thick insitu concrete with formwork to edges, to falls, tamped finish and trowelled edge	**405**	**805**

REPAIR POTHOLES TO FOOTPATH CAUSED BY BY SALT DAMAGE, SNOW CLEARING, WATER DAMAGE

	Patches (number)	
SOLUTION	1	2
Repair pothole in macadam or asphalt paving	£	£
Small holes up to $0.12m^2$	**94**	**115**
Large holes up to $1m^2$	**150**	**230**

DAMAGE CAUSED AS SNOW MELTS, LOCALISED FLOODING OCCURS

SOLUTION

3 BEDROOM SEMI DETACHED HOUSE (APPROXIMATELY 40M² GROUND FLOOR AREA)

Replace floor finishes damaged by water	£
Take up flooring, clean floors, lay carpet and vinyl sheet flooring	**5370**
Clean external brickwork to 1.5m high	**690**
Dry house including heating and disinfecting	**2650**

REPLACE MISSING ROOF TILES

SOLUTION

	Tiles/slates in One Location (number)			
Replace missing/broken tiles/slates	1	2	5	6
	£	£	£	£
Plain clay tile or concrete interlocking tile	285	305	325	330
Natural slate	290	315	340	350
Resecure tiles/slates	280	290	305	310

REBUILD DAMAGED CHIMNEYS

SOLUTION

	Pots per Stack	RANGE		
		£		£
Rebuild stack 1m high, replace 450mm high pots	1	2170	to	2760
	2	2970	to	3750
	4	4340	to	5130
Rebuild stack 1m high, replace 900mm high pots	1	2370	to	2970
	2	3360	to	4150
	4	5130	to	5930
Rebuild stack 2m high, replace 450mm high pots	1	2970	to	3750
	2	4340	to	5520
	4	5130	to	6520
Rebuild stack 2m high, replace 900mm high pots	1	3150	to	3950
	2	4740	to	5930
	4	5930	to	7300

REPLACE MISSING OR DAMAGED POTS

SOLUTION

	Pots per Stack		
Replace pots and flaunching	1	2	4
	£	£	£
450mm high pot	760	930	1270
900mm high pot	960	1330	2070

CRACKS IN EXTERNAL BRICKWORK

SOLUTION	Length of Crack (m)	£	RANGE Quality of Bricks	£
Cut out brickwork and replace with new brickwork at low level (no scaffolding required)	1	135	to	190
	2	210	to	325
	3	290	to	450
	5	445	to	650
Cut out brickwork and replace with new brickwork at high level (scaffolding required)	1	155	to	230
	2	240	to	380
	3	335	to	490
	5	490	to	700

	Length of Crack (m)			
	1 £	2 £	3 £	5 £
Pointing at low level				
Cut out crack and repoint to match existing	86	95	105	145
Pointing at high level				
Cut out crack and repoint to match existing	115	130	145	175

REPAIRS TO DOORS AND WINDOWS

SOLUTION	Single Items £
Doors	
Ease door without removal	68
Take down door, ease, adjust and rehang	82
Take down door, shave 12mm from bottom edge and rehang	82
Remove door, shave sides and top and bottom edges to fit opening, rehang	115
Ease and adjust door and frame of any size, adjust door stops, refix architrave and frame, overhaul ironmongery and leave in good working order	110
Windows	
Ease and adjust casement or sash window, overhaul ironmongery, renew beads with putty and sprigs, adjust stops and beads	110

CRACKS IN CEILINGS OR WALLS

SOLUTION

Repair cracks in ceiling

	Length of Crack (m)			
	1	2	3	5
	£	£	£	£
Rake out and fill in crack in plaster to ceiling not exceeding 75mm wide	105	115	120	135
Rake out and refill crack in plaster to wall	67	74	81	93

REPAIR BROKEN DRAINS

SOLUTION

Replace broken length of vitrified or plastic pipe

	Length of Pipe (m)			
	1	2	3	5
	£	£	£	£
100mm diameter pipe				
Excavate through soft surface, average excavation depth 500mm deep, replace pipe, make good ground	150	230	310	405
Excavate through concrete or paving or tarmac surface, average excavation depth 500mm deep, replace pipe, make good surface to match existing	210	355	425	710
Excavate through soft surface, average excavation depth 1000mm deep, replace pipe, make good ground	180	295	410	640
Excavate through concrete or paving or tarmac surface, average excavation depth 1000mm deep, replace pipe, make good surface to match existing	240	415	595	950
150mm pipe				
Excavate through soft surface, average excavation depth 500mm deep, replace pipe, make good ground	180	300	425	575
Excavate through concrete or paving or tarmac surface, average excavation depth 500mm deep, replace pipe, make good surface to match existing	240	425	520	880

REPAIR BROKEN DRAINS
150mm pipe (Continued)

	Length of Pipe (m)			
	1	2	3	5
	£	£	£	£
Excavate through soft surface, average excavation depth 1000mm deep, replace pipe, make good ground	215	360	435	735
Excavate through concrete or paving or tarmac surface, average excavation depth 1000mm deep, replace pipe, make good surface to match existing	275	410	620	1040

PART 3

3:1 COSTING ASSUMPTIONS

Costs in this guide are for completing the work described as an individual job. They include contractors' overheads, scaffolding, where applicable, and VAT. They exclude any temporary works, contingencies and any fees that may be applicable.

The level of costs for the type of work envisaged by this guide are likely to be very sensitive to the context under which the work is procured, the quantity and complexity of the permanent work required and the degree of temporary works needed to achieve it.

The cost of building work is influenced by a wide range of factors, which vary with the individual circumstances of the client, the work, the location and the contractor. No two contractors are likely to charge exactly the same price for an item of work. The information in this guide can therefore only be a reasonable indication of the costs involved in carrying out the work described.

Material and component prices used in this guide are prices for small quantities without trade discounts. Discounts available on manufacturers' list prices will vary from supplier to supplier, and for different purchasers.

The prices contained within this guide are intended to apply to building modifications carried out generally within the United Kingdom (ie. they are based on a national average level). It will be recognised that price levels vary throughout the United Kingdom. In order to provide some guidance on regional pricing levels, the regional factors from the BCIS Study of Location Factors are reproduced in Part 3.3. The

Study of Location Factors is based on a survey of prices in new building schemes.

The items have been priced individually, that is, as if there was only one item of repair identified which required action, following a survey.

- The works as a whole will be carried out or managed by a small independent builder or specialist tradesman.
- One item of repair work will be carried out to a dwelling. Should more than one item of repair be necessary to a dwelling then there may be cost savings on the rates provided. For example, an elevation may require total repointing and the roof on that elevation may require reroofing. The scaffolding cost will therefore be reduced, as erecting and dismantling would be included in the guide in both rates.
- The modification work will be procured via some form of competitive process unless it is of a very specialist nature.
- A call out charge has been included in the rates where work is of a minor nature and labour time is less than a full or half day. This rate varies, depending upon the trade.
- The modifications will be carried out in areas of the premises that can be isolated whilst work is carried out and to which contractors are allowed reasonably clear and unrestricted access.
- The work can be undertaken during normal construction industry working hours.
- Adequate and practical working space will be made available for the execution of the modifications and

for the temporary storage of materials and items of equipment.
* Water and domestic power will be provided free of charge.

Although the above criteria set the basis of costs, the prices and estimates in the guide have been compiled to reflect the general nature of modification work, which tends to be small items of work of either a specialist or multi-trade nature, executed at disparate locations within existing premises, generally under less than ideal working conditions.

Savings in on-costs may be achieved where it is possible to arrange for more than one item of repair work to be programmed and undertaken as part of a single repair scheme.

Additional costs may occur in situations where work has to be carried out in areas of the premises which are constantly occupied and cannot be closed off from the occupants, or where operational use has to be preserved. Additional expense cost is also likely where specific constraints are imposed on the contractor such as restrictions on:
* Access
* Working space
* Storage of materials and equipment
* Removal of debris
* Hours of working
* Noise, dust, vibration
* Method of working, sequencing, phasing etc.

The degree of additional cost will depend on the severity of the constraints imposed and the user of the guide will need to assess their likely effect on both labour productivity and the temporary works needed (see also below) and adjust the estimate they are preparing accordingly.

The quantity and complexity of the modification work to be executed will be significant factors in the cost of the work.

It is likely, with the repair works envisaged by this guide, that materials and components will often be needed in small quantities. The benefits of economies of scale will therefore be experienced where work can be organised on a scale that allows materials to be purchased in larger volumes.

Where only a very small amount of permanent work is required at one location, its real cost per unit quantity may be significantly higher than it would be if a larger amount were needed. This is not just because the materials for small volumes of work have to be ordered at 'small quantity' prices but also because the relatively fixed labour costs in travelling to the location, preparation (setting out, positioning materials etc.) and final clearing away are still incurred and can significantly inflate the cost per unit quantity executed. For example, the price for replacing one light switch has included additional charges, as an electrician will be obliged to journey to the location to carry out work that will take a relatively small amount of time. There may be a minimum flat charge of say £50 or £75 for such work (referred to in some contexts as a 'call out charge'). On the other hand, if five or six light switches need to be repositioned then the impact of the 'call out charge' is lessened because it starts to be absorbed by the cost of the greater quantity of work that is required.

The work becomes more complex to carry out if it is in a difficult position (eg. working at heights or on upper floors) with restricted access and lack of working space or if it is of an exceptionally high standard or quality. The prices and estimates in this Guide generally allow for work which could be considered to be of average complexity only, with a range of prices being given in the tables, where relevant, to illustrate normal differences in specified standard or quality.

Where only small quantities of work are required, the fixed cost elements of any temporary works needed (dust screens, protective barriers etc.) can be a very significant part of the total cost of the work.

The prices and estimates in this guide do not include any allowances for temporary works, other than minor incidental supports and formwork where they are needed in excavation work, forming openings and concrete work. All other temporary work is considered as being part of 'preliminaries'. The exception to this is scaffolding, where costs have been included in the rates, where appropriate.

Additions of 20% on labour resource costs and 10% on material and plant resource costs have been made for Establishment Charges (office overheads) and Profit to all prices in this Guide. The amounts these percentages generate are thought to be similar to those a prudent contractor would include to cover the costs of running a business and to allow for a reasonable profit.

An allowance of 12% has been made in the prices in this guide for Preliminaries (site overheads). Scaffolding, where required, has been priced additionally.

The extent of preliminaries will depend on the context of the job. They will vary widely according to the specific terms of the contract entered into as well as such criteria as the size, complexity and location of the project; the accessibility of the work; the amount of temporary works required; any restrictions imposed on working hours and practices; the feasibility and degree to which mechanical plant and equipment can be used; safety, health and welfare requirements.

No allowance has been made for Contingencies in the prices or estimates in this guide.

No allowance has been made in the prices and estimates within this guide for any Fees whatsoever.

Generally, the repairs, alterations and adaptations covered by this publication and which are contracted out are currently subject to VAT. All figures shown in the guide include VAT, at the current standard-rate of 17.5%.

The prices in this guide allow for work to be carried out during normal working hours. Extra cost will be incurred if work needs to be carried out in the evenings or at weekends.

The level of additional costs will vary depending on the working practices of the contractor but the nationally agreed overtime rates for building workers given below will give some indication.

Overtime	Basic Rates plus
Weekday or Saturday	
- First four hours	50%
- After first four hours	100%
Sunday	100%
Night Work (Permanent night working)	
Monday – Friday	25%
Weekends	100%

Where the term 'Prime Cost' (or its abbreviation 'PC') is used in this guide in relation to a material or component, the value it refers to represents the list price charged by the supplier excluding VAT, delivery charges and discounts. VAT has been added to the PC in the final rates.

The prices in this guide have been compiled on the basis that normal levels of wastage will be experienced. However, it is possible with the class of work envisaged by this guide that some forms of direct waste would be more difficult to control. Also, a greater than normal amount of indirect waste may occur where only a very small quantity of a material or component is needed but it can only be supplied in standard can or pack sizes and charged accordingly.

It is probable that the debris and waste arising from the type of works envisaged by this guide will be left on site or disposed of by the contractor, dependent on the type of waste. For larger repair work, skips will be provided by the contractor and will be classified as active waste (containing organic material and matter such as paint and timber). Therefore, where items in the guide include for disposal (eg. demolitions and excavations), an allowance has been included for skip hire for the removal of active waste. In smaller items of replacement (eg. renewal of ironmongery, sanitary appliances and the like) disposal is deemed to be covered by overheads.

3:2 WHERE TO GET HELP –

USEFUL CONTACTS

1. Professional Bodies

The Royal Institution of Chartered Surveyors, 12 Great George Street, Parliament Square, London SW1P 3AD
Telephone: +44 (0)870 333 1600
Fax: +44 (0)20 7334 3811
E-mail: contactrics@rics.org
Web Site: http://www.rics.org/

The RICS have published a number of free guides to help with homebuying and homeowner issues. Topics covered include buying and selling a home, extending your home, party walls, subsidence and flooding. The guides can be downloaded from www.rics.org/Practiceareas/Property/helping_hand.htm.

RICS Find a Surveyor Service
To find a surveyor in your area:
Telephone: +44 (0)870 333 1600
Web Site: http://www.ricsfirms.com/
E-mail: contactrics@rics.org

The Royal Institute of British Architects, 66 Portland Place, London W1B 1AD
Telephone: +44 (0)20 7580 5533
Fax: +44 (0)20 7255 1541
Web Site: www.architecture.com

The Institution of Structural Engineers, 11 Upper Belgrave Street, London SW1X 8BH
Telephone: +44 (0)20 7235 4535
Fax: +44 (0)20 7235 4294
Web Site:
http://www.istructe.org.uk/

The Federation of Master Builders, Gordon Fisher House, 14-15 Great James Street,
London, WC1N 3DP
Telephone: +44 (0)20 7242 7583
Fax: +44 (0)20 7404 0296

E-mail: central@fmb.org.uk
Web Site: www.fmb.org.uk

2. Party Walls

The Royal Institution of Chartered Surveyors, 12 Great George Street, Parliament Square, London SW1P 3AD

RICS Party Wall Guidance –
Web site: http://www.rics.org/partywalls

RICS Party Walls Helpline –
Telephone: +44 (0)870 333 1600

The helpline will put you in touch with an experienced, local RICS surveyor who will provide you with up to 30 minutes free advice.

3. Contracts for Building Works

The Joint Contracts Tribunal Limited
Web site: www.jctltd.co.uk/stylesheet.asp?file=492003233614
MW 05: Agreement for Minor Building Work

HO/B 99: Building Contract for Home Owner/Occupier (where the client deals directly with the builder)

HO/C 01: Building Contract for Home Owner/Occupier (who has appointed a consultant)

HO/RM 02: Contract for Home Repairs and Maintenance

HG(A) 02: Agreement for Housing Grant Works

4. Book Shops

RIBA Bookshops
Telephone: +44 (0)20 7256 7222
Fax: +44 (0)20 7374 8500
Email: sales@ribabooks.com

RICS Books
Tel: +44 (0)870 333 1600
(press option 2)
Fax: +44 (0)20 7334 3851
Email: mailorder@rics.org
Web site: http://www.ricsbooks.com

CIP Limited
Telephone: +44 (0)870 078 4400
Fax: +44 (0)870 078 4401
Email: sales@cip-books.com

5. Builders Federation

The National Federation of Builders
National Office, 55 Tufton Street,
London, SW1P 3QL
Telephone: +44 (0)870 8989 091
Fax: +44 (0)870 8989 096
Email: national@builders.org.uk
Web site: http://www.builders.
org.uk

6. Trade Federations

Painters & Decorators
Painting & Decorating Association,
Head Office, 32 Coton Road, Nuneaton,
Warwickshire CV11 5TW
Telephone: 024 7635 3776
Fax: 024 7635 4513
Web site:
http://www.paintingdecoratingassociati
on.co.uk/

Electrical Contractors
The Electrical Contractors' Association
(ECA)
ECA Head Office
ESCA House, 34 Palace Court, London,
W2 4HY
Telephone: +44 (0)20 7313 4800
Fax: +44 (0)20 7221 7344
Web site: http://www.eca.co.uk/

Plumbers
Association of Plumbing and Heating
Contractors (APHC)
14 Ensign House
Ensign Business Centre
Westwood Way
Coventry
CV4 8JA
Telephone: +44(0)24 7647 0626
Fax: +44(0)24 7647 0942
Website:
http://www.competentpersonsscheme.
co.uk

3:3 LOCATION FACTORS

The prices in this guide are average UK prices. The map overleaf shows regional pricing factors which indicate the general variability of pricing levels around the country. The factors are taken from the BCIS Study of Location Factors.

Adjusting for Location

The following examples show how to adjust the prices for a 3 x 3m single storey extension with one window.

Single storey extension as Page 177   **£21000**

	Factor	£
Scotland	1.04	**21840**
North West	0.92	**19320**
North	1.01	**21210**
Yorkshire & Humberside	0.99	**20790**
East Midlands	0.94	**19740**
West Midlands	0.93	**19530**
Wales	0.96	**20160**
East Anglia	0.98	**20580**
South East	1.05	**22050**
Greater London	1.14	**23940**
South West	0.98	**20580**
Northern Ireland	0.67	**14070**

Scotland
1.04

N.Ireland
0.67

North
1.01

Yorkshire &
Humberside
0.99

North
West
0.92

East Midlands
0.94

West Midlands
0.93

East Anglia
0.98

Wales
0.96

GL
1.14

South West
0.98

South East
1.05

3:4 INFLATION INDICES

The costs in this guide have been priced at fourth quarter 2007 price level.

The table below provides percentage adjustments on the costs of the estimated work from the price level in the guide to when the work is anticipated to be carried out on site.

Percentages figures all updated from 4Q07 Quarter		Percentage update
1Q08	(January, February, March)	1.012
2Q08	(April, May, June)	1.024
3Q08	(July, August, September)	1.044
4Q08	(October, November, December)	1.056
1Q09	(January, February, March)	1.068
2Q09	(April, May, June)	1.088
3Q09	(July, August, September)	1.108
4Q09	(October, November, December)	1.124

Adjusting for Inflation

The following examples show how to adjust the prices for a 3 x 3m single storey extension with one window.

Single storey extension as Page 177   **£21000**

Estimated date construction:	Inflation percentage		Revised Project Cost
November 2008	(4Q08)	1.056	£22180
March 2009	(1Q09)	1.068	£22430
September 2009	(3Q09)	1.108	£23270

3:5 HOUSE TYPES

The following diagrams have been produced to indicate the types of houses used in the production of various tables in the guide which give costs for whole house, elevations, floors, rooms etc.

Terraced House

Semi-Detached House

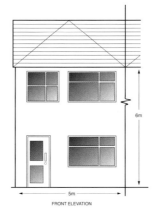

Detached House

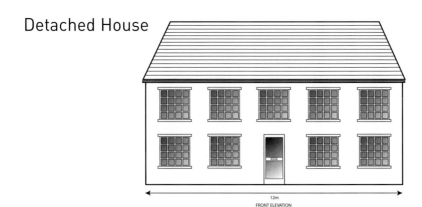

GLOSSARY

Architraves – timber moulding around door and window openings.

Battens – Wood strips onto which something is fitted. *For example:* roof tiles.

Beads – A small moulding covering a join.

Blown or Live Plaster – Plaster which has come away from the wall having lost its bond.

Brick Bond – The arrangement of bricks built to ensure the walls stability. *For example:* stretcher bond, Flemish bond.

Cavity Wall – The outside wall of the property, made up of an inner and outer layer or 'skin' with a void (cavity) between, often filled with insulation.

Contingencies or Contingency Sum – A sum of money allowed in your budget, on top of the agreed quote from the contractor, to allow for unforeseen works. An amount, either expressed as a percentage of the work or a lump sum. This will be for work that has not been included in the specification or shown on the drawings, but it may be advisable to allow a figure in case unknown items are encountered.
For example: The works may include replacing some floorboards. However when the old boards are removed, the joists supporting may be rotten and require replacing. The contractor will not be aware, until the boards are lifted, that the joists are rotten, and he will therefore not have included a sum in his quote to cover this work.

Coping – A protective capping at the top of a wall. *For example:* precast concrete coping.

Dpc, 'Damp Proof Course' – An impervious membrane built into brickwork to prevent movement of water through the brickwork. *For example:* laid about two brick courses above the ground, around window and door openings, made of hessian based bitumen felt, slate, etc.

Distribution Board – A unit containing switches, circuit breakers, fuses etc, which protect the electrical circuits in a property.

Eaves - An overhang of the roof beyond the wall below.

Estimate – An approximate price for one part or all of the work. This is sometimes used to mean quotation (see Page 193).

Fanlight – A window over an internal door to provide natural light into the corridor.

Flashing – A metal sheet used to deflect water and prevent ingress. *For example:* at the junction between the roof and wall

Flaunching – A cement mortar fillet at the top of a chimney stack, around the pots.

Flush Door – A door that has completely flat faces.

Foundations – A concrete or brick construction under walls, which provides support to those walls and structure above.

Gable – The upper part of an outer wall at the end of a pitched roof.

Grout – A material that fills the joints in wall and floor tiles and helps to prevent water ingress.

Hardcore – This is a material of broken bricks etc, which is laid under concrete beds or in soakaways.

Header Tank – A small open cistern (tank) that feeds water to a central heating system.

Herringbone Strutting – A zigzag pattern of timber that is fixed between joists to provide additional support.

Hip – The line adjoining parts of a pitched roof at the external angle of a building.

Hip Tile – A shaped roof tile which covers the hip.

Hipped Roof – A pitched roof whose ends are also pitched.

Insitu – Work which is constructed on site rather than constructed off site and brought into the works.

Ironmongery – Fittings installed to doors and windows to allow them to operate. *For example:* locks, bolts.

Joist – A support for floor and ceiling.

Knotting – A varnish to stabilise knots in wood.

Location Factors –Prices for work vary from region to region. The prices in this book are average UK prices and adjustments should be made on estimates for the location of the work.

Lintel – Concrete, steel or timber beam over an opening to support a wall above.

Making Good – The finishing touches that bring work up to scratch.

Manholes – A construction of brick, concrete or pvc that is situated in the ground where down pipes enter the underground drainage system or where there is a bend or junction in the underground system. The manhole will have a removable cover and the pipe will be open in order that inspections can be made.

Mullion – A vertical post in a window, dividing the window into parts.

Newel – Vertical post at the top and bottom of a staircase.

Nosing – The rounded end to stair tread. This projects beyond the riser.

Pantile - A curved 's' shaped or 'u' shaped roof tile.

PC Sum (Prime Cost Sum) – A sum of money allowed for an item of work or materials supplied by the client. *For example:* installation of a fire alarm system by a specialist already selected by the client, or the cost of a bathroom suite to be purchased by the client.

Pebble Dash – Wall finish with stones bedded in a rendered external wall.

Pitch – The slope of a roof.

Plain Tile – A flat rectangular roof tile.

Plasterboard – Prefabricated sheets of plaster, which are used for walls and ceilings.

Prefabricated – An item of the works made off site and brought onto the site. *For example:* roof truss.

Preliminaries – These are costs for items that are required to carry out the contract other than the actual construction costs. *For example:* travelling costs, the hire of scaffolding or other items of plant (e.g. cement mixers), office and other administrative charges.

Provisional Sum – An amount included in the contract sum/agreed quote for additional works that are not fully specified. *For example:* fitted units to a bedroom are required but the design/materials are not finalised at the time the contract is agreed. By inserting a reasonable sum, the contractor can allow for his overheads and include these works into his programme.

Purlin – A horizontal beam part of the way up the rafters. This helps to prevent the roof sagging.

Quote/Quotation – The price offered by the contractor to do the work.

Rafters – Roof timbers that rise from the eaves to the ridge to support a pitched roof.

Render – A coating of cement and sand applied to the face of an external wall.

Retention – A sum of money set aside by the client (you) from the contract sum until the works are completed to your satisfaction.

Ridge – The top apex of a pitched roof.

Ridge Tile – A tile, commonly half round, which is laid along the ridge, bedded in cement mortar.

Ring Main – The power circuit for electrical sockets in the property.

Riser (to stairs) – The upright part of a stair between treads.

Riser (water) – The vertical water pipe from the mains.

Rising Damp – Water that has come from below ground and rises up through the masonry by capillary action.

Roof Truss – A prefabricated structural timber framework to support the roof.

RSJ – 'Rolled steel joist'. A steel beam.

Sarking Felt – A waterproof felt under the roof tile battens.

Screed – A layer of fine concrete, which is used to provide a smooth surface prior to laying a floor finish.

Septic tank – An underground chamber, which collects the foul water from the property via waste and drain pipes.

Sill – The bottom horizontal member of a door or window frame.

Skim – The thin finishing coat of plaster that provides a smooth finish for decoration etc.

Soakaways – An excavated hole filled with hardcore to collect the rainwater from roofs taken through drain pipes into this pit.

Stack – The vertical pipe that carries waste water from toilets, baths, sinks etc to the drainage system.

String – The sloping board that carries the treads and risers of a staircase.

T & G boarding – T & G or tongued and grooved boarding is the traditional softwood flooring construction when the boards are jointed together.

Trap – A curved section of drain that holds water and provides a seal that prevents any odours returning into the room.

Tread – The horizontal part of a tread that is used to walk up and down the staircase.

TRV – Thermostatic radiator valve. This valve regulates the temperature of the radiator.

Underpinning – A method of supporting the existing external walls by excavating under the existing foundations and providing additional foundations.

Variations – These are work items that arise during the construction that were not allowed for in the quote. *For example:* during replacement of some floor boards, the joists below are found to be rotten. The quote only allowed for replacing the boards, the replacement of the joists is therefore a variation.

Verge – The edge of the pitched roof at the end of the property with a gable. The verge runs from the eaves to the ridge.

Verge Tile – The tiles at the end of the roof, running from the eaves to the ridge. These tiles are bedded in cement mortar.

INDEX